26-38

FERRUCCIO BUSONI IN HIS LIBRARY
From a hitherto unpublished photograph in the possession of the translator

FERRUCCIO BUSONI

THE ESSENCE OF MUSIC

AND OTHER PAPERS

Translated from the German
by Rosamond Ley

DOVER PUBLICATIONS, INC., NEW YORK

Published in Canada by General Publishing Company, Limited, 30 Lesmill Road, Don Mills, Toronto,
Ontario.

Published in the United Kingdom by Constable
and Company, Limited, 10 Orange Street, London
W. C. 2.

This Dover edition, first published in 1965, is an
unabridged republication of the work first published in 1957 by the Rockliff Publishing Corpora-
tion, London. This new edition is published by
special arrangement with Barrie and Rockliff.

The German papers translated herein were originally published under the titles *Von der Einheit
der Musik* and *Wesen und Einheit der Musik*.

Library of Congress Catalog Card Number: 65-26072

Manufactured in the United States of America

Dover Publications, Inc.
180 Varick Street
New York, N. Y. 10014

CONTENTS

v

CONTENTS

It seems fitting that "The Oneness of Music" should be put at the beginning and "The Essence of Music" at the end of this book, for in the latter article Busoni writes: "My earlier realisation of the Oneness of music might pass as a premonition of what I set myself to formulate here." This line of vision can be traced all through the book and culminates in "The Essence of Music".

The footnotes which are indicated by asterisks and daggers are translations of the editor's notes in the revised German edition. Those indicated by superior figures are Busoni's own, except where it is expressly stated that they are the translator's notes.

THE ESSENCE AND ONENESS OF MUSIC

THE ONENESS OF MUSIC AND THE POSSIBILITIES OF THE OPERA*

THE time has come to recognise the whole phenomenon of music as a "oneness" and no longer to split it up according to its purpose, form, and sound-medium. It should be recognised from two premises exclusively, that of its content and that of its quality.

By purpose, I mean one of the three realms of opera, Church and concert, and by form, the song, dance, fugue, or sonata; by sound-medium I mean the choice of human voices or instruments, and amongst these are included the orchestra, quartet and pianoforte, or the manifold combinations of all those mentioned.

Music remains, wherever and in whatever form it appears, exclusively music and nothing else, and it only passes over into a special category through the description given to it by the title and the superscription, or the text to which it is put, and the situation in which one places it. Therefore, there is no music which can be stamped and recognised as being Church

* The Essay in the first edition of Busoni's *Von der Einheit der Musik* originally bore the title "Entwurf eines Vorwortes zur Partitur des Doktor Faust, enthaltend einige Betrachtungen über die Möglichkeit der Oper", written in Berlin, August 1921. The Preface to "The Score of *Doktor Faust*" was first published at the end of this essay (left out in the text here) and was written in July 1922. Both works appeared together later as a separate book with the title *Concerning the Possibilities of the Opera and Concerning the Score of Doktor Faust* (Breitkopf & Härtel, 1926).

The change in the title should make clear the special problem of the essay. The work about the score of *Doktor Faust* is to be found in Part III of this edition.

music, and I am certain that no one listening to some pieces out of Mozart's Requiem or Beethoven's Great Mass would feel and define these works as sacred if title and text were kept a secret from the listener. The Gregorian Chant, with its lapidary unisons and complete absence of harmony, is absolutely bound up with the Church in our conception and we feel it as Church music, just as much as we feel it in the style of Palestrina, yet love-songs in the time of Palestrina seem so very like an Offertorium that they could easily be mistaken for such and only the text and the occasion distinguish one from the other.

At the time of the formal establishment of the ritual chant by Pope Gregory there was no other kind of music, and it is to be supposed that a romance from this epoch would not sound very different from what we believe today to be truly authentic Church music. Our feeling about "theatre music" is just the same for, through a bad habit, a certain convention has been adopted generally, which we accept as being "theatrical" because we know that this convention comes from the opera. But it is just this opera convention which is the formula that least concerns the music; it is mostly a trick, which, like others originating in the theatre, is imitated by all and used as a concession to the singers, often used in a perplexity in order to compensate for a lack of higher expression or in order to find a skilful mode of transition.

In *Konzert Musik*—and wherever music exists as a living art—from Haydn downwards we find reminiscences of the theatre. At times in the more cheerful moments of the "smaller" Beethoven whole long stretches follow the *opera buffa* in expression and movement.

Recognising this does not minimise the worth of these passages. Art is a transmission of life, and the theatre does this more comprehensively than the other arts; therefore it is natural that living music should be allied to the theatre.

This Oneness, which I advance as a first principle, exists already and is sustained almost uninterruptedly in the works of Bach and Mozart; these two are still the strongest and most enduring musical personalities in our present-day art of music—and this fact in the end must also be recognised. Amongst Bach's works the little deviations in expression and style are most frequently to be traced back to the instrument which executes the music assigned to it. There is little difference to be found between an organ piece and a piece for clavecin—allowances being made for the instrument and the player—but we hear the same Bach with the one as with the other. The instinct of "Oneness" made Bach use the same music as a work for choir or for an organ piece, and he continually carries his ideas from one instrument to another, from "Church" music to "chamber" music. If the Evangelist from the St. Matthew Passion were put on the stage, one would be so flabbergasted one would be obliged to admit that nothing more theatrical had ever been conceived than this strictly religious music. But every one of Mozart's operas is a pure symphonic score and there is something of an opera scene in each quartet. The gifted theorist Momigny made the experiment of putting words in the style of an aria in *opera seria* to the first movement of Mozart's D minor Quartet; through this experiment, when listening to the piece thus newly interpreted (and otherwise not changed by a note) we experience the effect of being thrown suddenly into the middle of a Mozart opera.

It is astonishing how little music has to do with human conventions (can one speak seriously of "court" music?) and thanks to its neutrality, how it fits and adapts itself everywhere. This makes it possible and understandable that Beethoven should have taken a movement originally written for a Court Cantata, making use of it later in the Finale of *Fidelio*, and extracted from the theme of an antiquated wind octet (a weak early work) the joyful strains which, also in *Fidelio*, celebrate the release of the prisoners. Through convention, the march, the dance, the Protestant chorale remain more unconditionally assigned to their purpose. In spite of this, in a symphony or sonata, marches and dances are not objected to, and are even passed over with approval, and in chamber music the chorale

3

is separated from its original destiny and used with artistic effect. In opera, the chorale appears chiefly as a quotation or symbol; although nothing in its "musical" nature (a leading part in minims and a pure four-part movement) points demonstrably to "religion". Therefore the differences of kind and class take place only in the preconceived idea of those concerned with the music.

It is, on the contrary, the content and the *quality* which make the music in itself different.

Invention and *atmosphere* compose the content, *form* and *shape* the quality. A piece may be easy or difficult, stirring or sustained, clear or obscure, full of artistic device or simple (the essential ability and the mastery of ideas and atmosphere are pre-supposed), but all this does not in the least prevent its being used as Church, theatre, or chamber music, although on the other hand, it is included in each one of these categories.

Hand in hand with the splitting up of music into types, there is also a scale in the valuation of music under apparently antagonistic headings, rather like a music tariff. Thus, in Germany, the symphony passes as the highest form and appearance in music, whilst the opera is a little despised. As if, in the *Magic Flute* both the men in armour's music was not more beautiful and more important than any grey string quartet from the second half of the nineteenth century! By this, I mean that it depends on the quality and not on the grade and class—and again, on how alive it is, on its vividness and power for new life and vigour. Music is surely an art of movement!

Having thus arrived at the recognition of the Oneness of music we have consciously looked at what was lasting or effective in the past. But our attitude is different from what it was before, and we can now see the possibilities in a new light, and rule and manage them differently and carry them still further. Not only do I believe that no inferior kind of music need be brought to mind by the opera, and that it will enjoy equal rights with other kinds of music (whereby its class will take a

4

higher rank but above all its particular class would be established) but—and I come to this conclusion without any hesitation at all—I expect that in the future the opera will be the chief, that is to say the universal and one form of musical expression and content. Music, which makes the unspoken eloquent and lifts human disturbances out of the depths in order to transport them to the imagination, finds in the opera primarily the creative space for its own expansion, but it will not portray outward incidents and visible occurrences. The outward incidents appeal to our eyes, the inner ones to our ears. Sight and hearing mutually complete, support, and illustrate one another, if the directing hand of the artist is able to hold them apart successfully, and to unite them. What, however, turns the scales in favour of my conclusion is the fact that opera conceals, united in itself, all the means and forms which otherwise only come into practice singly in music. It allows them and requires them. It gives the opportunity for making use of them collectively or in groups. The domain of the opera extends over the simple song, march, and dance tunes, to the most complicated counterpoint, from the song to the orchestra, from the "worldly" to the "spiritual"—and still further—the unlimited space over which it disposes qualifies it to take in every kind and style of music and to reflect every mood.

In addition to this the tasks are increased by the theatre. It demands more intensive expression, a more tensely strung bow, a more powerful diction than is enough for music in other cases.

Beethoven, who surely had at his disposal a strong and supremely good symphonic ability, composed four versions of his overture to *Fidelio*. For use in the theatre, the sovereign composer of symphonies was only satisfied with the last one of these settings. In point of fact the so-called "third" *Leonora* Overture surpasses all the first movements of his symphonies, with the exception perhaps, of the Ninth. And even in this final and inspired setting, the episode of human passion formed from the Florestan Aria would in the theatre have been able to stream forth in a still wider spirit if it had been written for the theatre; which objection—raised against Beethoven—is no hasty criticism but a lawful challenge.

Undoubtedly, the theatre increases the difficulty. A choral fugue in an oratorio, for example, can extend as far as the execution and contrapuntal skill of the composer reach. On the stage, with equally capable construction it must at the same time suit the theatrical situation without the one acquisition doing harm to the others. For—and this seems to me to be essential—an opera score, whilst fitting the action, should show detached from it a complete musical picture; comparable to a suit of armour which, intended for the envelopment of human bodies, in itself exhibits a gratifying picture, a valuable work in material, form and artistic execution. In fact—and it may sound paradoxical!—the composition of opera leads us back to purer and more absolute music because by means of the suggested future and banishment of everything illustrative, only those elements which are organically suitable to music attain their own rights: the content, feeling, and the form, synonymous with spirit, heart, and understanding. In the same measure that the theatre demands the heightened expression, it has the power to subdue harshnesses. Therefore, a series of dissonances that is almost unbearable on the pianoforte, is already intelligible in the orchestra, but in the theatre it becomes merely a characteristic nuance which is put up with and passes without opposition. The demand for accents, increased by the stage, is so very much stronger. As a natural consequence, through the intensified qualities and the universality gained by the opera, a decrease in productiveness must follow because—as a final conclusion—a composer, a creator, brings to a single opera all that moves him, all that swims before his eyes, all that is within his powers to achieve: he is a musical Dante, a musical Divine Comedy.

The objection will be made that the theatre coarsens the expression and cripples the form. To overcome this objection it is enough to put Figaro's Hochzeit against it; as rules should not

6

be deduced from imperfect but from perfect examples. But by this it should not be "vinta la causa" (as happens in *Figaro*); on the contrary, in order to exhaust the case, some considerations and reasons must still be brought forward and this I shall do as follows.

Above all, the opera should not be identified with the spoken drama. More than this, they should be distinguished from one another like man and wife. It is, with the opera, a question of "a musical work of the combined arts" as against the Bayreuth conception of it as "a work of the combined arts" (if Wagner is to be brought forward now and for ever, in order to set the mind of the 1921 reader at rest by naming the standard on which he places reliance). To me, the all-important condition seems to be the choice of the libretto. While for the drama there are almost boundless possibilities of material, it seems that for the opera the only suitable subjects are such as could not exist or reach complete expression without music—which demand music and only become complete through it. Therefore, the choice of subject matter for opera is strictly limited, according to my view of the musical stage of the future as something finer than we have yet known. To achieve this aim it is imperative that the public, which it also concerns, should allow itself to be educated and should educate itself. It should first of all free itself from the ideas and conditions of the spoken drama as from things opposed to the opera: it must also free itself from the idea of the performance of a cheap amusement and from the demand for and expectation of a sensational drama, the intrigues of which while they are mentally exciting can yet be experienced by the public without danger from the stalls. Sensual or sexual music (which consists in a kind of persistence in the intoxication of sound and thus plays on the keyboard of the nerves) is obviously out of place owing to the very nature of this art, which is purely abstract. Yet unfortunately today such music must still be pointed out as particularly absurd and unworthy. It should be cleared of all traditional theatre routine

7

and be apart from business interests as also from social conventions. In order to follow on from old mystery plays, the opera should be made into a rare half-religious and elevating ceremony which is at the same time stimulating and entertaining, just as the service of God amongst many of the oldest and most primitive people found expression in the dance, and just as the Catholic Church still goes some way towards making spectacle out of homage to the Deity and so can make good use of music, costume, choreography and theatrical mysticism —often with the finest taste.

The Magic Flute comes nearest to this ideal. It unites instruction and entertainment with a solemn spectacle to which entrancing music is added, or rather permeates all this and holds it together. The Magic Flute, to my mind, is "absolute" opera and it is surprising that, in Germany especially, it has not been set up as a sign-post for the opera. Eckermann informs us that "Goethe, who made a continuation of it but found no composer who could treat the subject suitably, admits that the first part (of Mozart's opera) is full of improbabilities and jests which not everyone can interpret and value, but in any case it must be admitted that the composer understood in a high degree the art of contrast and how to convey big theatrical effects thereby". But this fine praise from an eminent man is not exhaustive. Shickaneder produced a libretto which contains music in itself and which positively demands its appearance. The magic flute and the magic chimes are already musical elements destined for sound. Besides this how cleverly the three women's voices and the three boys' voices are arranged in the libretto, and how the "miracle" calls forth the music, and how the "trial by fire and water" relies on the evocative magic of music. The two armoured watchmen too in front of the "trial" gateway both make their admonishments in the rhythm of a very old choral melody. Drama, morality and action join hands here in order to set this seal of their alliance on the music.

Goethe had thought of his second Faust half "operatically". He wished (it would seem from his own communications)

8

that the choruses should be *sung* throughout, and he expressed the opinion that it would be very difficult to perform Helena's part because it required a "tragic actress" as well as a prima donna. If this plan had been realised in one of the poems of equal rank in form, we should have had a second model for what I am here trying to pave the way. For in the "Second Faust" music is needed everywhere, it is indispensable, the poem cannot do without it, and it must come to the help of the performance of the play as light helps the inspection of a picture. (This proves the helplessness of theatre directors, and the inadequacy of most of the *Faust* music.)

Let us take, as an opposite example, a "drama" like *La Dame aux Camélias* or *La Tosca*. In a play written originally as pure drama, we are not seized with a longing for the missing music, the piece (good or bad) is, in itself, understandable and complete without music, so much so that one forgets that there is such a thing as music in or out of the theatre. One can judge from this what an enormity was committed in wishing to make operas out of these plays! If mysticism were in the blood of the Latin people as much as the theatre is, in the future they might be unrivalled "operists" (this word formation is perhaps permissible as it serves the sense.) But there, where they live, the sun is too clear and the twilight calls them to occupations which in those lands are destitute of all mysticism. They demand Life from the stage, as with justice it is demanded everywhere, but they demand the life that they lead themselves. Only they commit the error of also putting it to music. Even the greatest succumb to this error. Verdi also succumbs to it, though his genius for climaxes, his pathos, and his choice of speed frequently succeed in making the music break through this confinement, even in the opera of intrigues.[1]

---

[1] The *Allgemeiner Musikalischer Anzeiger* (a weekly paper published by Tobias Haslinger) in 1839 quotes the following sentences from an article in April 1803:

The Marriage of Figaro. To arrange a play of intrigue as an opera is certainly not a happy idea, indeed one may say that in its nature it is

Pathos, like sound, is already nearer to music than any cadence made to sound like it; rhetoric and declamation are half song. In a drama which is unfavourable to music Verdi's sure instinct knew how to prevent the music being completely stifled, and in *Otello*, for example, he intersperses a drinking song, a mandoline solo, an evening prayer, and a romance (that of the willow), as musical numbers and cleverly turns them to the best advantage. Through these "insertions" *Otello* becomes almost an opera. A similar contrivance so that the musical lyric shall not be lost, is the "love-duet" (the love-duet of the Italian opera) but I condemn it unconditionally. A love-duet on the public stage is not only shameless but absolutely untrue, not untrue in the beautiful and right feeling of artistic transmission, but altogether wrong and fictitious besides being ridiculous. A situation is shown in the

---

completely opposed to opera. Beaumarchais in his comedy *La folle journée* uses some pleasing *bons mots* and ambiguous witticisms to set off some scenically effective and dramatically attractive situations; but for music he has done nothing; on the contrary he has practically barred the way to it by building up the material to a thoroughly clear and equivocally satirical conclusion which is utterly unconnected with music. Perhaps Mozart only took this subject because there happened to be no other at hand which bore the stamp of celebrity and he could unashamedly attempt it since genius such as his does not easily admit impossibility.

I first heard these opinions and the expression "play of intrigue" as applied to opera when I had already sent my present study to the printer. That these views written in the year 1803 should coincide so perfectly with what I have written has moved me to incorporate them here to illustrate my point.

Contemporary voices are also raised in inevitable demands. Dr. Massino Zanotti of Rome wrote lately (in *Melos*, August 1921): "I believe in the possibility of an artificial Italian Theatre where the action is limited to a minimum of what is necessary for the intensification of lyrical feeling [he means "what is necessary for an unfolding of the musical content"]. I believe in a theatre where the action will itself constitute the lyrical intensification so that the music will always remain free, free music, music in the true sense of the word."

I must also refer to a very stimulating article by Herman Kessers in the periodical *Feuer* (also August 1921) which, in its way, sheds a light in advance on much that I have written here.

frame of the opera which in any other costume or century or
any other surroundings displays the same well-known physiognomy (such is love!) which interests no one, least of all the
lovers themselves who can feel nothing because their own
experiences teach them something quite different. There is
nothing worse to see and to hear than a small man and a large
lady raving together melodiously and holding each other's
hands. What felicity and judgment Goethe showed in his
circumnavigation of this rock, in the conversation between
Faust and Gretchen. Domestic information and: "How dost
thou stand with regard to religion?" When action begins
words cease. Eroticism is no subject for art but a concern of
life. Those who feel the inclination should experience it; but
not represent it or read a representation of it and least of all set
it to music. Anyone who has made a third in the company of
lovers will have felt this to be painful. It is to a whole audience
that this happens during a love duet.

In the older operas there is no love-duet.

The old composers had still got taste, in the same way that
they still had measure and proportion and knew how to make
use of them at the right time. In Cimarosa, Mozart, Rossini,
this balance amazes us because we have almost completely
unlearnt it and to a certain extent it grew out of the nature and
form of the libretto. A theatrical composition which was meant
for the opera was planned throughout quite differently from
one intended as spoken drama. In the action which the recitative (musically inconspicuous) knit together, the music (for the
sake of which the arrangement was made) was conceded
"stages", resting points which summed up the situation reached
and at which it could widen out into arias and ensemble
movements. The text for these stages was generally made up of
two quatrains, so that it was entrusted to the composer according to inspiration and mood to work out either a short or a
long piece of music from these two quatrains. After which, the
interrupted action again took its course. How unnatural!
Certainly, very unnatural! What can and shall the opera be

other than something unnatural? What could produce a "natural" effect in opera? When developing the opera we must start consciously from these premises which constitute the basis of every dramatic composition. So what I desire from an opera text is not only that it conjures up music, but that it allows room for it to expand. The word allows music to cease, but on the other hand it does not compel it to expand unnecessarily in its service, if the music has had its say.

By means of the catchword (abridgment) it is possible for opera to obviate this inconvenience. The *Schlagwort* in the opera takes the place of the tirade in the drama. To make this clear, here is a constructed example:

In Drama or in Music Drama
THE OLD MAN Where are you going?
THE YOUNG MAN To the rocky gorge.
THE OLD MAN Oh, be warned, many go there but never come back; evil spirits lurk behind the rocks to set snares for the unwary traveller: evil men, perhaps, who knows? They say tall Kaspar has been seen there surrounded by a good dozen despairing faces whom he seems to rule. And have you not heard of old Barbel, the witch who lights her fire at midnight so that all around the rocks glow with a blood-red light? Wild animals also live there: crawling poison on which your foot steps unintentionally, and which will revenge itself on your young blood.

The young man expresses his fearlessness with corresponding minuteness and with no fewer embellishments than in the foregoing speech and he adorns all this with long tales about the bold pranks of the born adventurer.

In place of this in Opera
O. MAN Where are you going?
Y. MAN To the rocky gorge.
O. MAN [*Horrified*] To the rocky gorge? Go not!

12

Y. MAN I fear nothing.

O. MAN I tell thee, go not. Danger threatens thee there.

Y. MAN Let me go [*Drawing away*]

O. MAN [*To himself*] Shall I ever see him again?

Just as the abridgment can sum up the inner part of the text of an opera, it can be transferred in a changed form to the action in general. In relation to the music it serves to create a situation rather than to give the reasons for it logically. An abridgment in the action might be, for example, in the entrance of the Rival. The onlooker simply recognises the Rival in the figure appearing. By this the situation is created. No matter from whence he comes or who he is. Anything else can be effected by costume and conduct. If the Rival appears in knight's attire we know at once that this second suitor is a nobleman; his possible advantages and his prerogatives in the competition become evident through his rank. I should call this the "optical" abridgment. After all, the sets are really nothing but a scenic abridgment. Forest, Church, Knight's Hall. And in this case (without our missing it) there is no connecting context. We do not see the path which leads through the town to the church and on to the forest and up to the castle into whose knightly hall we step. Those are the tasks and crafts of the cinematograph and in no way belong to the opera.

The abridgment, therefore, is an invaluable tool for the opera because there the audience is burdened with the task of looking, thinking and hearing at the same time. An average audience however—and the public, in gross, presents itself as such—only has the capacity to follow one of these three at a time. Therefore this counterpoint of attention which is demanded should be simplified by allowing speech and music to retire where action has the chief rôle (a duel, for example); by putting music and action in the background when a thought is being communicated; by action and speech both being unassuming when music spins its threads. The opera is play, poem and music in one. Sounds and pictures maintain their

13

position in it, to such an extent that this characteristic already separates it sharply from the spoken drama, which exists without any spectacle and without music. This reason alone makes the limitation of the poem a condition.

But there is yet another reason: that of proportion. One reckons that the text when set to music fills nearly three times as much time as when it is spoken. For this reason an opera text should be planned so as to be about two-thirds shorter than the text of a play. Once again, I maintain that a good opera score, independently of the text, should be able to establish itself musically and the poem should further this aim in every way. (The theatre all too quickly swallows the nourishment which makes it capable of living, and is always greedy for new food. Only the soundness and cleanness of the score is able, after its short existence on the stage is over, to preserve an opera as an artistic monument for posterity. Many an opera which passed for dead, has been brought to light again by the excellence of the score.) On this account much may be prescribed by the composer to the poet, but almost nothing by the poet to the composer. In the end an ideal union is found only in the solution that a composer should be his own poet. In this way he will be granted, without opposition, the right to shorten, to supplement, or to arrange the words and the scenes, just as the musical circumstances demand during the course of the composition. Because of this, I am obliged to smile when unknown writers offer me their libretti with a preamble something like this: "I hear that you favour oriental fairy stories. My text treats of such and I hope you will put it to music." Think, it is as if somebody had written to me: "I do not know you but have heard that you are considering marriage and that you favour fair women. I send you my daughter, she is fair and I hope she will become your wife."

I should like also to establish the fact that the opera as a musical composition always consisted in a series of short, concise pieces and that it will never be able to exist in any other form.

Neither human conception nor reception lasts long enough for threads to be spun uninterruptedly for three or four hours on end. This cutting up into smaller pieces was shown quite openly by the old composers, the new vainly hide it under the mask of rejecting "full closes", thereby losing the rhythmic structures, and the rhythmic structure is an organic condition of the musical structure, as breathing is to human beings and animals. ("More air!" a Goethe of music would have exclaimed.) It is indeed not by accident that separate numbers can be taken from the "endless chain" of the *Ring* and used in the concert hall—Waldweben, Walkürenritt, Feuerzauber, and so on. We can notice in this constellation how Wagner's musical instinct caught hold of those "stages" which in earlier operas, as Aria and Ensemble, denoted that the drama was taking breath. But in this case it happens that they are produced by what is instrumental and not by what is vocal. I have spoken in another place about the countless conditions and forces which are drawn in and put into activity in the performance of an opera. With regard to this question—by way of comparison—Goethe writes in his preface to *Farbenlehre*: "For as really scarcely half of a good play can be put on paper, and by far the greater part of it must be left to the glamour of the stage, the personality of the actor, the power of his voice, the characteristics of his movements, indeed to the mind and good mood of the audience; so . . ." I cannot do otherwise here than oppose a completely contrary view to that of my deeply honoured Master. For my part I think that the performance can help a weak play very much and that with good luck complete justice may be done to a good play. But every expectation and hope of seeing an unusual and exceptional play performed exhaustively, must be renounced. "The mind and good mood of the spectators" may be influenced by the temperature of one single evening, indeed decide it. The positive value of a work cannot be changed in the least by the mind or mood or by any other view or criticism—and a serious discussion about the public in this connection does not seem to me to be admissible. No, as soon as one wishes to work seriously, it is advisable not to join in any compromise with the stage. The opera which stands for everything improbable, unbelievable and impossible, may claim the right to do so on the surest and best of grounds.

With my three fundamental theories, the three-part division of whole tones, "Young Classicism", and *the transformation of the opera through the perception of the inherent Oneness of music*, important material has been collected for further action. To the youngest I cry: Build up! But do not content yourselves any longer with self-complacent experiments and the glory of the success of the season, which flares up quickly; but turn towards the perfection of the work seriously and joyfully. "Only he who looks towards the future looks cheerfully."

II

THE FUTURE OF MUSIC

OPEN LETTER TO HANS PFITZNER*

Zürich, June 1917

Honoured Friend,

You pay me the honour of expressing your opinion openly about my little book. But whereas what I wrote was intended to be of an abstract and conciliatory nature, and to be aimed at no one individually, you make a controversial reply which is openly directed against one person, changing the general into the particular, the temporary and the personal.

By the title alone, "The Danger of Futurism", you lead your reader astray by heaping on my name, in the eyes of the public, all the weaknesses and faults with which you could possibly reproach a certain group of people—a group from which I am far removed.

The word "Futurism" is not used on any page of my little book. I have never attached myself to a sect—Futurism, a movement of the present time, could have no connection with my arguments.

You consider it a defect in my work "that I have not drawn up something like an aesthetic law", while the whole tenor of the little book is against the drawing up of general rules as being a hindrance to a free art.

But also, you believe that your view of the questions started by me lies nearer to many people than mine. You say: "It will,

* Hans Pfitzner published a pamphlet called "Futuristengefahr" ("The Danger of Futurism") in the *Süddeutsche Monatshefte* which was chiefly aimed against the *Entwurf einer neuen Aesthetik der Tonkunst* ("New Aesthetic of Music"). This "open letter" was a reply published in the *Vossische Zeitung*, Berlin, June 1917.

perhaps, not be unwelcome to these to learn something more in accordance with their views."

It is just for these people that my book is written, so that for once they may hear something from "the other side" as well.

But whilst I have never questioned your art publicly either with your followers or with anyone else, you draw an unjust and ugly picture of me from which they get to know me for the first time.

You proclaim me openly as a disowner and despiser of all great composers of the past without quoting any of my sentences as proof of such a monstrous accusation; but you rely solely on "the impression as a whole, which one has from the reading of this little book".

I must, first of all, refer you and your readers to my edition of Bach's *Well-tempered Clavier*, which certainly cannot appear to be written in a tone of disavowal or disrespect.

When I exclaim, on page 10 of my little book: "Mozart, the Seeker and the Finder, the great man with the child-like heart, we gaze in astonishment at him, we hang on him", no one will be able to misunderstand the absolute reverence which is manifest therein.

I am a worshipper of Form! I have remained sufficiently a Latin for that.

But I demand—no! the organism of art demands—that every idea fashions its own form for itself; the organism—not I—revolts against having one single form for all ideas; today especially and how much more in the coming centuries.

The "law-givers" (and you know who and what is intended by this symbolic word) have constructed their formulas after the creations of the masters, the latter go in front, the former follow after, and at a good distance. "The creator [p. 31 of my book] only strives for perfection and as he brings this into harmony with his individuality a new law arises unintentionally."

From the "magic child", music, I still look for what is yet undreamt of, and towards which my "desire" goes: the all-human and the super-human. It is the desire which acts as the first mainspring of realisation. Therefore, I cannot and should not like to say precisely what form such a development will take; no more than, thousands of years since, the longing of men to be able to fly could describe the apparatus which today fulfils this longing.

If my "promises" remind you of Jules Verne's romances do not forget that much technical fantasy in these books has now become fact.

But how do you describe the course of life of the "magic child" music?—"After [see p. 10] it had grown to a wonderfully vigorous and healthy baby with his nurse from the Netherlands, he passed happy times in the Italian boarding school, and after a hundred and fifty years is now at home in our Germany where, as a beautiful and strong youth, it is to be hoped he will thrive for a long time yet".

Consider, honoured friend, how with time even the most beautiful and strongest youth matures to an old man, and for the maintenance of a powerful race, cross-breeding is a well-known expedient.

I believe you are too honest intentionally to misrepresent my book, which is well-meant and full of peace, as harmful teaching; therefore a misunderstanding must exist, which I consider it my duty—confronted by such an esteemed opponent—to put right with these few lines.

YOUNG CLASSICISM*

Zürich, January 1920

Dear Herr Paul Bekker,

I have read your article—"Impotence or Potency"—with interest and sympathy, and for much that is said I am heartily indebted to you. Even if Pfitzner cannot awaken my interest

---

* This letter to Paul Bekker was a personal one which arose out of the controversy between Pfitzner and Busoni. It was first published in the *Frankfurter Zeitung*, 7th February 1920, and then reprinted in the Busoni number of *Anbruch*, 1921.

and sympathy to the same extent—and indeed he does not wish to do so—yet I cannot quite overcome the fear that there is some misunderstanding between him and what he attacks; not only do I believe that all of us whose intentions are honest strive for the best and utmost possible perfection in music—a common starting-point which should abolish all antagonism—but I believe further that there are certainly dissimilarities in the compositions of today, that is to say dissimilarities in talent! But not chasms separating them; I believe they are more alike than we suppose or will allow ourselves to believe. (Dissimilarity in the attitude of mind is another thing altogether. . . .)

At all times there were—must have been—artists who clung to the last tradition and others who sought to free themselves from it. This twilight condition seems to me to be the stable one; dawn and the full light of day are considerations of perspective for historians who gather them together and gladly arrive at results.

The appearance also of isolated experiments which stand out as caricature is a usual concomitant of evolution; the strange, ape-like forward-springing gestures of those who stand for something; either defiance or rebellion, satire or foolishness. This type has appeared again in greater numbers during the last fifteen years and it strikes one all the more forcibly after the standstill of the 'eighties which remains quite isolated in the history of art. Unfortunately it coincided with my own youth. Exaggeration, with which the beginner today already makes his first appearance, is becoming general and portends the end of such a period; and the next step is that which inclines towards Young Classicism (which opposition is bound to stimulate).

By "Young Classicism" I mean the mastery, the sifting and the turning to account of all the gains of previous experiments and their inclusion in strong and beautiful forms.

This art will be old and new at the same time at first. We are steering in that direction, luckily, consciously or unconsciously, willingly or unwillingly.

But this art, in order to arise intact in its newness, so that it will mean a genuine result to the historian, will be founded on many hypotheses which today are not yet fully apprehended. I feel the idea of Oneness in music as one of the most important of these as yet uncomprehended truths.

I mean the idea that music is music, in and for itself, and nothing else, and that it is not split up into different classes: apart from cases where words, title, situations and meanings which are brought in entirely from outside, obviously put it into different categories. There is no music which is Church music in itself, but only absolute music to which sacred words are put or which is performed in church. If you change the text, the music apparently changes also. If you take the text away altogether, there remains (illusorily) a symphonic movement; join words to a movement from a string quartet and an operatic scena grows out of it. If you play the first movement of the "Eroica" Symphony to an American-Indian film, the music will appear so changed that you will not recognise it. For this reason you should not use the terms "instrumental music" and the "true symphonic composer" which you let fall in your article about chamber symphonies. I do not permit myself to criticise you but I am under the impression that by using these words you surely place yourself nearer to Pfitzner than you intend.

With "Young Classicism" I include the definite departure from what is thematic and the return to melody again as the ruler of all voices and all emotions (not in the sense of a pleasing motive) and as the bearer of the idea and the begetter of harmony, in short, the most highly developed (not the most complicated) polyphony.

A third point not less important, is the casting off of what is "sensuous" and the renunciation of subjectivity (the road to objectivity, which means the author standing back from his work, a purifying road, a hard way, a trial of fire and water) and the re-conquest of serenity (*serenitas*). Neither Beethoven's wry smile nor Zarathustra's "liberating laugh" but the smile of wisdom, of divinity and absolute music. Not profundity, and personal feeling and metaphysics, but Music which is absolute, distilled, and never under a mask of figures and ideas which are borrowed from other spheres.

Human sentiment, but not human affairs, and this, too, expressed within the limits of what is artistic.

The measurements of what is artistic do not refer only to proportions, to the boundaries of what is beautiful and the preservation of taste, they mean above all not assigning to art tasks which lie outside its nature. Description in music, for instance.

This is what I think. Can this, to return to what was first said, can this opinion be contested by honest people? Do I not much rather hold out my hands to universal understanding? Is it possible that these theories could be considered injurious and dangerous on the one side and as retrograde and compromising on the other side? I entrust them to you.

F. B.

My dear boy,* already more than two years ago, as you know, I threw the expression "Young Classicism" into the world and prophesied popularity for it. For me there is something strange about it, for today the expression is circulated and there is nobody who knows who coined it. So it is said at times that Busoni also follows the "Young Classicism"...! It is not necessary to be a prophet to imagine it. After a seriously large number of experiments from the original "Secessionists" to the "Anti-Secessionists" and finally, after the manner of crowds, to separate groups getting further apart, the necessity for a comprehensive certainty in style must be met.

But, as with everything else, I was misunderstood about this also, for the masses look upon Classicism as upon something turning back. This is confirmed in painting by the rehabilitation of Ingres for instance who, a Master himself, is a terrible

* From a letter to his son, 18th June 1921, taken from Debusmann's *Ferruccio Busoni* (1948).

example of dead forms (the impression made by this opinion is intended to be sharp).

My idea is (this is feeling, personal necessity rather than constructed principle) that Young Classicism signifies completion in a double sense; completion as perfection and completion as a close. The conclusion of previous experiments.

SIMPLICITY OF MUSIC IN THE FUTURE*

IN the editions I possess of Poe, there are many carefully arranged, good, and characteristic portraits of the poet to be found. But a picture of Poe by Manet, etched with a few strokes, sums up all the other pictures and is exhaustive. Should not music also try to express only what is most important with a few notes, set down in a masterly fashion? Does my *Brautwahl* with its full score of seven hundred pages achieve more than *Figaro* with its six accompanying wind instruments? It seems to me that the refinement of economy is the next aim after the refinement of prodigality has been learnt. Perhaps this will be the third phase of the first book in the history of music; then new starting-points and new means may have to arise to produce in sound the longing which is the pedal note of human polyphony. This might lead eventually to freeing humanity from what is most difficult.

THE NEW HARMONY†

Chicago, January 1911

BETWEEN Minneapolis and New York I have some hours of Sunday repose. The travelling bag, which contains my work, lies at the station; there is no pianoforte in the room, so I am thrown on my own thoughts. With your permission I will impart one of them to you.

* From the "Aufzeichnungen" in *Von der Einheit der Musik* (1922).
† Written in Chicago, January 1911, for the periodical *Signale*, Berlin.

The present-day harmony and that of the future interest me as they do the musical world and with a similar intensity. At present there is a searching and groping but I see the roads. There are five in all and as yet no composer has walked up to the end of any of them.

The first new harmonic system rests upon chord formation according to customary scales. (Debussy, out of 113 scales which I have compiled, only employs the whole-tone scale, and that only in the melody.)

By the symmetrical inversion of the harmonic order Bernhard Ziehn shows me the second way.

Keeping the voices independent of each other in polyphonic compositions produces the third road. (I have, as an experiment, constructed a five-part fugue in which every voice is in a different key so that the harmony flows in quite new chord successions.)

A fourth road is anarchy, an arbitrary placing of intervals, next and over one another, according to mood and taste. Arnold Schönberg is trying it; but already he is beginning to turn round in a circle.

The fifth will be the birth of a new key system which will include all the four afore-mentioned ways.

I believe this list is as clear as it is complete; it contains enough material to fill an extensive volume. This is left for the latest theorist. For every good theory can be expressed in a short sentence, whereas every fundamental sentence contains the stuff for an extension as long as you please. The world, to be sure, usually only allows itself to be convinced through works of several volumes.

CONCERNING HARMONY*

Berlin, January 1922

Dear Herr Windisch,

I have already pointed out and emphasised the fact several

---

* These arguments about "Harmony" originally appeared as an open letter, written in Berlin, 17th January 1922, and first published in *Melos*.

times, that in our art the mind, the skill and the content set the standard for the estimation and the endurance of a work. A change has been brought about amongst the more progressive critics of today and a standard set which does not differentiate according to the value of a piece but according to the direction in which it moves; it rejects good things moving in older directions, and honours bad productions with the newest tendencies.

But there is an art which stands "jenseits von Gut und Böse" (beyond good and evil), and which remains a great art in every age; before this art critics of the most advanced kind bow down instinctively as before that of Bach or Beethoven and nolens volens ... Wagner. These critics are concerned with the living, and amongst these their discriminations divide what is old and what is present-day with the sharpness of a knife and those in the former category are turned aside, the latter honoured. Now a piece is not good because it is new and (this is the comical thing) it is not new because it appears without form or beauty![1]

There are three things which are made use of by neo-expressionism: harmony, hysteria and temperamental gestures.

The harmony can do no other than draw from the twelve half-tones standing at our disposal, all possible combinations of which have been tried and made use of. The only remaining characteristic is the removal of the consonance, leaving the dissonance unresolved. Whereby the harmony is stunted as a means of expression, and the individuality of the author effaced: to me, at least, the harmonic structure of all neo-expressionists sounds alike, whatever the composer's name may be. This is especially the case in the excessive use of octaves and fifths which one meets everywhere.

The "hysteria" is maintained by using short disconnected forms of sighs and of runs, in the obstinate repetition of one or more sounds, in fading away and using the highest of the high

[1] In the end one can recognise in such a piece a relic from Wagner, a dis-guised Debussy, shameless salon and dance music.

and the deepest of the deep sounds, in the pauses and in the accumulation of different rhythms within one bar. All available means of expression are used as far as they can have a place appointed for them within the structure of a composition.

The "temperamental gestures" appear chiefly in orchestral works on which, by a semblance of polyphony, still more restlessness is imprinted.

Generally speaking, it is a characteristic that at the commencement of a piece, all means and formulas appear immediately, in full strength and are exhausted, so that every possibility for making any further stress during the course of the composition is forestalled. In general, renunciation is the order of the day in the place of enrichment; to all appearances more has been joined on to the work already done, but in reality this work is blasted by what is joined on to it so that no intermediary road leads to a new starting-point.

There is a pleasant anecdote in which the Shah of Persia, during a visit to foggy London, was asked whether it was true that they prayed to the sun in his country. The Shah is said to have replied: "If you knew the sun you would also pray to it."

Stravinsky told me once, through a third person, that he found it strange to hear that I admired the German classical composers. Whereupon I commissioned the third person to reply to Stravinsky that if he knew the classical composers he would also value them. (I have not been able to ascertain if the reply was delivered.)

But why does harmony (called cacophony by opposers and atonality by adherents) play such a very privileged and decisive rôle? Because it is produced on a system which demands neither skill, nor imagination, nor feeling, and gives everyone the possibility of the right to stagger backwards and forwards at will. But new harmony could only arise naturally from the foundation of an extremely cultivated polyphony and establish a right for its appearance; this requires strict tuition and a considerable mastery of melody. This system does not exclude the

26

possibility of retaining the traditional harmonic changes where they are in place, and where they would evoke contrast; it does not exclude the use of simple formulas for simple thoughts. And there is certainly a difference between setting a simple "Good morning" to music, and an ironical greeting, or a greeting quite hostilely felt. It is not sensible, with a simple "Good morning" to put harmony which is not simple. I have replied already to the objection that what, to our ears, may sound strange today, may sound simple to other ears in the future. To allow for every differentiation is only possible on these lines. I know too that I have occasioned a great deal of misunderstanding through my little book *A New Aesthetic of Music*. I retract no sentence which stands there, but against certain interpretations of my sentences I must defend myself. *By "freedom of form" I never meant formlessness, by "Oneness in music" I did not mean an illogical and zigzag harmony, by the "right of individuality" I never meant the noisy expression of any blunderer.*

If a doctor advises the enjoyment of wine, he does not wish his patient to become a drunkard. The state of freedom must not be confused with anarchy, because in anarchy every individual is threatened by the other. Magnanimity is not the mania of prodigality and free love is not prostitution. More-over, a good idea is not an artistic creation, someone with talent is not a master; a seed of corn, however strong and fruit-ful it may be, produces no harvest for a long time.

Far from advising against every effective resource being taken up in the workshop of our possibilities, I only desire that it shall be applied aesthetically and intelligently; that the pro-portions of the measures, sounds and intervals shall be artistic-ally distributed, and that a creation, however it is planned or formed, in its final completion should rise to the rank of a classic in the original sense of the word. I think I have expressed myself sufficiently clearly and remain,

Yours,

F. B.

FUTURISM IN MUSIC*

IN the spring of this year Futurism in Music was preached in the Paris paper *La Liberté*—the number reached me late. The leader of the movement preserves his *incognito* but openly expresses his opinion in a manifesto:

The composers of today who are modern devotees of the past only deserve our contempt, for they labour in vain, composing original works with worn-out means. . . . Hear then the aesthetic laws of Futurism. These laws consist, in fact, of nothing more than the division of the octave into fifty intervals. The idea is physical in origin and has been considered repeatedly. Know that shortly we shall have completed "chromatic" pianofortes, stringed instruments, harps, in fact a complete "chromatic" orchestra. Simultaneously with the futuristic composer's work, the work for the realisation of it is carried out. In the shadows of the workshops, the forms of families of instruments arise, whose unsuspected perfection will make the perfect reproduction of futuristic compositions possible.

At the same time similar news comes to me from Moscow where musical Nihilists are at work.

That is right. It pleases me, and I stood on this side long ago, if only as a theorist. Already in the year 1906 I proposed the division of the octave into thirty-six intervals, two rows of tripartite tones (each tone divided into three) at a distance of a semitone from one another.[1]

"The universal instrument" has already been made in America: the electric dynamic organ. It cost a million, remained untouched and fell into ruins.

* Written in Berlin, September 1912; appeared in *Pan*.
[1] Compare the "Bericht über Dritteltöne" (1922).

There are just two questions left:

> First, before we begin a new way, can we do everything
> in the old way as well as it has been done in the past?
> Secondly, in addition to this have we the talent?

The first question is disposed of in concise style in the manifesto. "We wish to approach music with a virgin soul. . . . We trample traditions under our feet. . . . The musical gods are dead. We soar with them no longer at the touch of their creations."

Until the curtain goes up we cannot say whether the answer to the second question will be in the affirmative.

Futurism must wait for that moment. Then it becomes the present. And the manifesto itself teaches: "The present is a vain idea; say 'it is' and already *it is no more. . . .*" *Tout passe.*

REPORT ON THE DIVISION OF THE
WHOLE TONE INTO THREE PARTS*

IF there is one thing which is just as bad as wishing to retard progress, it is this: forcing it stupidly. It is sixteen years since I drew up, theoretically, a possible system for the division of tones into three (a tripartite tone) and I have not yet decided to make a conclusive publication of it. Why? Because I am conscious that a responsibility falls on me as the originator of the proposition. The possibility of practical experiment is still withheld from me; and I know very well that I could only put forward my ideas with exactitude through a series of conscientious and thoroughly tried-out investigations. I have accomplished little. In New York an intelligent and aged pianoforte maker from Trentino rebuilt for me an old harmonium which had three manuals, giving it two rows of tripartite tones at a distance of a semitone from one another. The arrangement of

* Written in Berlin and published in *Melos*, August 1922.

the intervals proved so impracticable that it was not possible to strike them easily one after the other, but still I had heard the new intervals. I played a chromatic scale in tripartite tones to a little circle of intelligent musical friends in the next room. The result, it was agreed, was that they thought they had heard an ordinary chromatic scale in semitones. This impression confirmed my supposition that the ear is able to separate tripartite tones one from another clearly, and not feel them as something like semitones out of tune. In order not to renounce the semitones, and consequently the minor third and perfect fifth, I had a second row of tripartite tones added to the first row at a distance of a semitone. Through this, every third tripartite tone preserves its semitone. The blending of both rows produces, of course, sixths of tones. Thus the melodic system becomes capable of considerably more power of expression, but it complicates the harmony so much that it demands a very strictly thought-out systematisation. This is still unborn and can only begin to exist through the ears. But according to my principle, progress implies an enrichment and not a lessening of means. Innovators without any head on their shoulders, begin with the rejection and obliteration of what already exists. I prefer to place the younger acquisition on what is existent. Therefore in the foregoing case I keep the semitones in the clear consciousness of their value in the power of expression, knowing that to relinquish them would be the most superficial tomfoolery.

The whole-tone scale with Debussy, and with Liszt before him, is like an anticipation of the whole-tone interval being filled in with the not yet existent tripartite whole-tone intervals. In this expectation the semitone is passed over. But only in the melodic parts; the accompanying harmony remains the one that has long been established. Therefore one does not destroy, one builds up! Time automatically rubs off what is wrong and unnecessary and automatically takes up what is good and beneficial in order to keep it. And the great and beautiful thrive.

MELODY OF THE FUTURE*

Melody is the watchword of the dilettanti; only ask them
what they mean.   SCHUMANN

Three things belong to composing, first of all melody;
then again melody; then finally, for the third time,
melody.   JADASSON, *Book of Instruction*

That something, greater than ourselves which does not so
much exist as seek existence, palpitating between being
and not being, how marvellous it is! It has worn the form
and visage of ten thousand different gods, sought a shape
for itself in stone, ivory and music, and wonderful
words. . . .   H. G. WELLS, *The New Machiavelli*

IT can be said—contradict it who may—that Wagner was the
first to use melody as a universal law. Before Wagner, this was
always "recognised".

The older art of composition neglects melody, the older the
art the more emphasised this is.

Unconsciously we feel the rule of another standard in the
classical works and we measure them with a smaller measure.

The broad sweep of the newer symphony diverges from the
music before Wagner. There, the eight bars still rule—with
short breaths on great heights—and what fills them out is of a
more primitive formation. With Beethoven it is most pronounced in his second period—the weakest of the three—in
the Fifth, the "Waldstein" Sonata and in the Three Quartets,
op. 59.

Again it might be said—again, contradict who may—that
in the first of Beethoven's creative periods feeling overcomes
helplessness, in the third period this same feeling, coming up
from the depths, drowns the acquired mastery.

In the middle period, on the other hand, feeling withdraws

* Published 2nd July 1912 in the *Zeitschrift für Musik*. The first sketch was
a letter to his wife, 15th March 1911.

before symphonic expansion and splendour of forms. This second period of Beethoven's is the exploitation of the strong ideas in the first period. The passionate defiance of the "Pathétique" remained the basis for ideas in all similar moods of sound during the following periods, from the Fifth Symphony onwards, only more expanded, adorned, and underlined. But the expansion stands in bad relationship to the extensiveness of the melodic element which gets lost on a kind of—what shall I say?—plateau of modulatory and figurative eloquence.

I am thinking, for example, of the exposition in the first movement of the "Appassionata" where the great rising and persistence in temperament takes the place of subject-matter. It is the thrilling eloquence—his own—the infectious conviction of the orator, instead of his theme, which affects the listener here; it has an effect on larger masses of people and makes a more sudden impact. Temperament puts a mask of more physical uncontrollability before thought and the emotion of feeling, that is without thought or feeling.

It has become a permanent commonplace in the history of music to reproach every composition, appearing for the first time, with a lack of melody. *Don Giovanni* met with that reproach on the occasion of the first performance in Berlin; it was the same with Beethoven's Violin Concerto, and with Wagner's music dramas. And again, the increase in technical discoveries is always put as the reason for decrease in melodic invention. It almost seems as if technical mastery could make its effects more through what is unusual, and melodic expression only through what is familiar. But, in fact, Mozart was a richer maker of melodies than his predecessors; Beethoven broader, more ingenious than Mozart; Wagner more luxuriant than Beethoven, if also less noble, more dependent, more material, more of a characteriser, less of a psychologist. It is against this materialism that a group of living composers is attempting to react.

Immateriality is the real essence of music that will ring out in a blossoming and sublime melody.

AN ATTEMPT AT A DEFINITION OF MELODY*

A ROW of repeated (1) ascending and descending (2) intervals which (3) organised and moving rhythmically (4) contains in itself a latent harmony and (5) which gives back a certain atmosphere of feeling; which can and does exist (6) independent of text for expression and (7) independent of accompanying voices for form; and in the performance of which the choice of pitch (8) and of instrument (9) exercise no change over its essence. (The nine arguments noted as numbers in brackets should be commented upon explanatorily.)

This "absolute" melody, at first a self-sufficient formation, united itself subsequently with the accompanying harmony, and later melted with it into oneness; out of this oneness the continually progressive poly-harmony aims to free and liberate itself.

It must be asserted here, in contradiction to a point of view which is deeply-rooted, that melody has expanded continuously, that it has grown in line and in capacity for expression, and that it must succeed in attaining universal command in composition.

PROPORTION†

THERE are three kinds of proportion which surpass all the rest in importance: measurement in time, contrast in sound, and relationships in modulation. And three subordinate ones: movement, sequence of intervals, and atmosphere.

It would be possible to write a detailed chapter about each of them, and a book about them collectively making use of existing and especially composed examples. The section on sequence of intervals leads directly to the system of melody which it is among my plans to draw up. Already in the year

* Draft published in *Von der Einheit der Musik*, 1922. The first sketch was a letter to his wife, 22nd July 1913.

† Written in Berlin, September 1922.

1915, I wrote in Part II of the *Well-tempered Clavier*: "In theoretical literature there is no book on melodic forms and it would be a valuable publication, if not in order to help towards the production of new and beautiful motives, at least in order to help in the 'recognition of beauty' when it already exists. Perhaps also to hinder a further growth of that demonstrably wrong, melodic formation, which, since Beethoven, has sometimes been met with even among the most highly esteemed German composers. It is even conceivable that in the future an aim, developed to the highest point of pre-eminence, may take the place in art of the instinct which is fading gradually and produce compositions of a quality as alive as those produced by inspiration. But in the compositions of the future (whatever the origin of the motive power) 'melody' should govern with absolute sway and in the perfected manifestation of it there will be a 'final' polyphony."

In order that "the aim may develop to the highest pre-eminence", it is necessary to examine the laws of proportion thoroughly. Looked at as laws and subsequently felt and practised freely as an acquired balance, they lend to the structure which they serve that durability which inspiration alone does not guarantee.

Conception is the same as gift. Intention a matter of character. Direction a sign of the epoch.

It is the form which first raises conception, intention and direction to the rank of a work of art. And inside the form, proportion is one of the strongest and most sensitive demands. In a later volume, which will treat of these questions, I hope to meet the reader again.

THE THEORY OF ORCHESTRATION*

ONE day lately I read an announcement of a publication, which was shortly forthcoming, of Berlioz' book on instru-

* Written for *Die Musik*, Berlin, November 1905.

mentation revised by Richard Strauss. It is to be hoped that this revision will avoid the fundamental defects of all instruction books on instrumentation up to the present, and in so far as a dumb book is able to teach a free and eloquent art, that it will accomplish this also. In my review of Breithaupt's book *Die Natürliche Klaviertechnik*, I remarked that every gifted artist forms his own technique, but there are however rules about things which everyone must avoid and others which everyone must make use of. This applies to instrumentation also. But what are these unchangeable rules?

Above all it must be emphasised and impressed upon the learner from the beginning, that there are two kinds of instrumentation: that which is demanded and directed by musical thought—absolute orchestration—and the instrumentalisation of what was originally only an abstract musical composition, or one conceived for another instrument. The first is the only genuine one, the second belongs to "arrangements". Nevertheless up to now there are more composers who transcribe for the orchestra than those who invent and feel purely orchestrally. Above all, I count Mozart, Weber, Wagner as the foremost "genuine" composers for orchestra, and in the first rank, Berlioz. Even Wagner lapses into orchestration, as for example in the working out of the *Meistersinger* Overture, and there he has endeavoured as clearly as possible to transcribe for orchestra an abstract musical composition. Beethoven almost always "orchestrates". To him the musical idea and the poetic human value are the most important things for him and the first to arise.

True, "orchestral moments" hover in places before everyone who plans an orchestral piece, yet they are mostly only moments and the learner is directed to these places for the manner in which to design the whole work with all the details. And these moments are constantly as follows: sustained horn notes, roll of kettledrums, flourishes on the trumpets—the childish maladies of instrumental writers. What comes in between is generally "arranged". It must be taught therefore that the orchestra is a single instrument, a connected organism in which all the organs are active at the same time. There is nothing more unorchestral than long passages for the strings or drawn-out passages for the woodwind, with no participation for the other instruments. Once in a way such writing can be employed as contrast, or as illustration to a special situation, and then not again. That is a "special" effect, and teachers of instrumentation generally busy themselves much too much with such "special effects". "Special effects", therefore—a third point—should be placed in an appendix, or better still, left to the imagination and individuality of the orchestrator who is already mature.

A fourth rule which I do not find even mentioned anywhere and which is yet always confirmed in all Mozart's and Wagner's scores, is that every instrument whether it is used singly or in groups, has to convey its passage with meaning from the beginning to the end, so that it always represents a separate picture. This is not only more beautiful but it sounds better.

The fifth: the woodwind, flutes, oboes, clarinets and bassoons are still always represented in storeys one after the other. But if the bassoons reach the lowest and the flutes the highest notes, one must not forget that the bassoon reaches up a whole octave into the compass of the flute, and that the clarinet reaches down deep into the bassoon's range of tone, and that for all woodwind there is a stratum of unison in existence: the octave

Ex.1

the common-room in which all the occupants of the different storeys meet together.

The sixth is to learn that necessary arrangement which, in the orchestra, takes over the function of "the pedals" in the pianoforte. At times one plays the pianoforte without pedal, yet the right foot is usually active, continually helpful, filling out and joining together, not to speak of the pronounced big pedal effects. This "right foot" is also indispensable in the orchestra. The teacher should devote a whole chapter to it.

A seventh chapter must deal with pianissimo and fortissimo. The rule exists, in spite of model examples to the contrary, that for pianissimo as few instruments and for fortissimo as many as possible should be used. Yet it is proved that one can effect a velvety-soft piano with trumpets and trombones and quite a brilliant forte without them.

That leads to an eighth chapter which I should like to call the "Dynamic Atmosphere" and which should afford the proof that the effect of the plane of intensity is relative and depends upon its surroundings.

The idea of the degree of intensity leads to an extraordinarily important ninth chapter—that which discusses sound proportions. A good score could be created in such a way that the sound gradations are included in it and allowed to be heard without special assistance from the executants. The "prominent" middle voice must be orchestrated, not sounded more loudly or more fully. The crescendo must take place through the arrangement of the instruments, the theme must shine forth of itself. A strict proportion should govern the doubling or trebling of the voices. If a doubled instrument does not reach high or low enough, one should put a substitute at once which is suitable in character and strength. With many voices there are different condition. and the sound-characteristics of the register are to be weighed precisely, and at the same time one must not forget the melodic design!

A tenth chapter could be called: "What is Necessity? What is Luxury?" They should be in the same relation to each other as the skeleton is to the flesh-covered body, as the naked body to the dressed, as the dress to the ornamentation. One learns first of all to put down necessities.

Finally, one learns that orchestral music is, in a pronounced sense, "public music", and that its effects are to be measured for that. As chamber music is allotted to intimate effects, virtuoso

37

music to the large and small salon, choral music to societies, festivals and special occasions, military music to streets and squares, orchestral music is stamped for the big public hall without which it cannot exist. It is after this fashion that I have in mind a book of instruction on instrumentation and it is to be hoped that the realisation of it will be made by Richard Strauss.

INSUFFICIENCY OF THE MEANS FOR MUSICAL EXPRESSION*

A CONVERSATION that I had a few days ago with two friends of mine, musicians, opened my eyes in many respects but chiefly to the insufficiency of the means for musical expression, especially with reference to the present-day orchestra. In fact even if the ideas of most of the living composers do not exceed the possibilities offered, and if our "Master" hardly knows how to manage the existing material, it is on the other hand not to be denied that:

1. The incompleteness of the orchestral instrument singly, as well as in the formation of the orchestra as a whole, hampers imagination and the power of creation.
2. Possibly there are musicians and will be musicians who, for sound effect, long to go far beyond the boundaries now drawn (that such musicians in the future will go beyond the boundaries of form, of harmony, indeed perhaps of the whole system of tonality, is now already more than an idea).

But it is to be feared a genius such as this could not succeed in carrying his conception into effect so long as the richer means desired are either not invented, or are not in regular use. So far as a short reflection and the use of what imagination

* Written to the editor of the *Musikalisches Wochenblatt* (E. W. Fritsch, New York), 14th November 1893, and found in Busoni's posthumous papers. The letter should have been published there but this cannot be ascertained.

nature has given me allows, I have tried to classify as follows necessary improvements that are possible and improvements not yet invented.

1. Instruments that are permanently in use only in large orchestras of the first rank. As for instance: English horn, bass clarinet, contra-bassoon, harps, bass tuba, Glockenspiel, three and four drums. Although today they cannot be replaced, they are not sufficient in an orchestra of instruments in general use.
2. Instruments used in isolated bars with decided success still count as exceptional means but are to be found permanently in small orchestras. Examples: The family of saxophones, the tenor tubas, the viola-alta, the cymbals (the gypsy cymbals); as far as I know the employment of the latter has not been tried at all yet.
3. Instruments which might be desired, and are capable of being perfected, or the number of which could be increased. Examples: A complete family of flutes, bass-oboes, soprano bassoons, low contra-bassoons, chromatic harps, pedal drums (which can perform passages and other things).
4. New instruments of the future. For example: A glocken-instrument, with a compass of six octaves with keyboard; filling out all gaps in the sound and in the technique of every individual instrument.

THE FUTURE OF OPERA*

THE sung word will always remain a convention on the stage, and a hindrance to any semblance of truth; to overcome this deadlock with any success a plot would have to be made in which the singers act what is incredible, fictitious, and improbable from the very start, so that one impossibility supports the

* Extracts from the *Entwurf einer neuen Aesthetik der Tonkunst*. Written in Berlin, March 1913.

other and both become possible and acceptable. . . . It is for this reason and because it disregards this most important principle from the beginning, that I look upon the so-called Italian "verismus" for the musical stage as untenable. . . .

On the other hand if the form of a plot accompanied by music and illustrated by song is considered without the text, it might produce a kind of "sung mime". . . .

It is necessary to be clear about a second point in connection with the question of the future of opera, namely: "At what moments is music indispensable on the stage?"

To this question the precise answer is: "During dances, marches, songs, and at the appearance of the supernatural in the action."

The idea of the supernatural as a theme follows, therefore, as a possibility for the future. And there is yet another: that the stage should be accepted openly as a pretence, as nothing but "acting" and sustained make-believe; with the idea of jest and unreality being contrasts to the seriousness and veracity of life. Then it is not out of place for the singers to declare their love and unload their hate and fall into a melodic duel, and hold on to high notes in pathetic outbursts. There it is in order for them to behave intentionally in a way contrary to life, instead of turning everything upside down unintentionally (as happens in our theatres now and particularly in opera).

The opera should take possession of the supernatural or un-natural as its only proper sphere of representation and feeling and should create a pretence world in such a way that life is reflected in either a magic or a comic mirror, presenting consciously that which is not to be found in real life. The magic mirror is for grand opera, the comic for light opera. And dances and masks and apparitions should be interwoven, so that the onlooker never loses sight of the charms of pretence or gives himself up to it as an actual experience.

The artist, if the control over his medium at certain moments is not to be lost, must not be moved when he wishes to move others, and in the same way the onlooker, if the artistic enjoyment is not to be debased to human participation, must never consider it as reality. The performer "acts", he does not experience. The onlooker, being incredulous, is thereby unimpeded in mental reception and keen enjoyment.

On such assumptions a future for the opera can well be expected. But the first and greatest obstacle for us will be, I fear, the public itself.

In my view the public has a thoroughly criminal attitude to the theatre for most people demand a strong human experience from the stage, no doubt because such experiences do not come into ordinary lives and also because they crave for excitement for which they lack the courage; and the stage deals out these excitements without involving the audience in the accompanying dangers and disasters and, above all, sparing them any exertion. For the public does not know and does not wish to know that in order to receive a work of art, half the work must be done by the receiver himself.

WHAT IS HAPPENING AT THE PRESENT TIME*

EVERYWHERE, not least in Germany, similar symptoms of revolution appear in musical endeavours. They are alike in all countries, and evidently the outbreak of this present-day movement is a post-war expression; in the sense of being transferred, new conditions bring about new manifestations, in art they call forth new expression and the supposed prerogative of the individual to proclaim it. The principle of one single individual is pushed forward; many even renounce this and hammer on the principle of freedom of opinion; the idea of establishing those of their predecessors is simply scorned. The older men,

* The first publication of an autograph manuscript, found among Busoni's posthumous papers, that has no date or title.

who appear to be liberal and open-minded, are in search of a seeming juvenescence in it, which they agree with and follow and which gives them the illusion that they are at the head of the movement. The youth of the demonstrators and the irregularity of their productions seem to be the outstanding features of the movement; gift and ability are only a secondary consideration, sometimes not considerations at all.

But the movement is too general and consolidated for it to be ignored, nor must it be so. It must be dealt with, the facts registered, and looked at as objectively as possible.

The seeds of these blossoms, however, were sown before the war. Schönberg, the Vienna Secessionist, Stravinsky, the Russian acrobat of sound, laid the foundation for misunderstandings which through over-trumping pass today for positive truths. A little book of mine published in 1906 but only read ten years later, in theory also misled many through a particular interpretation being applied to it in the war. And here over-trumping came forward in the place of the power to convince, and I felt both annoyed and satisfied because, however crooked the result, I could see an effect which came from my teaching. I speak of it in the past because already in the year 1920 (this time in Zürich) I foresaw the end of expressionism, then at the zenith of its importance. From it we have got some possibilities which we add gratefully to our useful means and of which we shall make use from time to time. There is a kernel of truth in each of the bigger movements, the error lies in emphasising this fact, for then one thinks and acts in an exclusive, exaggeratedly intolerant and ridiculous way.

Inborn gift and acquired knowledge will always give the casting vote in the valuation and permanency of a work of art. The "direction" remains a transitory sign of the time from which it sprang, and if the particular type reaches perfection then it becomes a "classic" and (without further dispute) is put into the existing stock of what is good. If it does not reach this perfection the type disappears as it came and it simply marks an "incident" in history which bore no result.

It depends therefore on the gift of the individual, on his self-discipline, self-renunciation, on the tenacious cultivation of his abilities, wherever something "lasting" is formed out of the "direction" he takes or in which he was set going. An achievement such as this cannot emanate simultaneously from a group of people aged about twenty. The craft requires too long a training for that, life too great a number of experiences.

The newcomers deceive themselves, too, in thinking they can break, or have broken, with all their predecessors. This is not the case, in spite of their unshakable conviction, for every child has a mother to whom it is still attached by the navel even after birth. These newest-comers are in fact less original than they themselves suppose. On the other hand it is undeniable that the eyes of the human being are set in such a way that he is obliged to look forward, for only then, if he lives in the present, is he passably competent to exist. It is a question of destiny if the times are confused and have indistinct and oscillating outlines. The creators who are sentenced to come into this confusion have to endure it. Therefore, unless he is narrow-minded, it is the duty and task of anyone who sees this confusion to bring light into these conditions, to differentiate and support wherever there is darkness, complication and oscillation. Besides this, in the development of the artist, whether it appears singly or as a whole group, a manifestation has been observed which changes the initial unruliness into quietude—often into the life of a Philistine. The man who is a considerable innovator at first, turns back and becomes a reformer. Think of Schumann, think of Beethoven. It is more consistent for those who have learnt about practically all that existed in the past, to be satisfied with it no longer and to devise something new; again it is also natural that the store of opposing ideas and energies in the young revolutionary should soon be exhausted and either languish through repetition or return to what is more normal through reaction. Thus it is preferable for a disturbed epoch to close on future order resulting from it; against this the storm gathers in a heavily laden atmosphere and makes the mariner uneasy.

Now there is an absolute, demonstrable beauty and perfection and there are things that please certain people at certain times and will be looked upon as beautiful by them. Whichever direction the work of art adopts it falls ultimately to one of two destinies, it either remains lost or becomes a classic, just as it happens to belong to the first or second species. Furthermore it is the direction that changes and the perfection that is permanent. The first is accidental and dependent, almost without importance, the second is important, independent and lawful. Not lawful in the sense of dry rules, but in relationship to itself.

The question is not: Is such and such different from the old? But rather: Is it just as good, is it much better than the old? And at intervals it happens that the answer to the latter question is in the affirmative, through either clarification or comparison, but only, and without exception, owing to the combination of gift and ability. It is to be supposed that among such a number of youths a personality will appear sometime—perhaps soon— who will show the revolution's good kernel in its complete circle; he will naturally rise to be a classic, thereby separating himself from his previous companions. It is to be supposed each thinks that this particular one is himself and in this way from among those who were once like-minded, adversaries arise later on. Already one can discern, among the groups, similar dispositions of the whole "school" as well as individuals to make a divergence—in the mass as well as singly (the school lacking a head). Both sides of an angle diverge more and more, the further they go. At first from inborn race characteristics, coming out of the darkness of nationality—the different countries dared not make themselves known to each other. Inside these countries the chosen one will become visible. At present, however, the Germanic people clearly hold more closely together; the Latin people the same; opposition and insufficient training are common to them all.

But on the whole, at all times, the rotation takes place and only what we had not experienced before causes us surprise. But these experiences must recur again at regular intervals of time and under unparalleled conditions. The whole preceding occurrence, for example, was disconcertingly present-day nearly a hundred years ago and was put down in the conversation between Mephistopheles and Baccalaureus (*Faust I*). Two hundred years before that Cervantes said the same thing. And he was hardly a Philistine any more than Goethe.

III

ABOUT HIMSELF AND HIS WORKS

SELF-CRITICISM*

NUN gibt es Fälle, wo ein Mann so von einem Erlebnis
erfüllt ist, dass er gedrängt füllt es darzustellen . . . er
greift zur schriftlichen Mitteilung—als Beichte; zur
übertragenen Form des gestalteten Bildes als Spiegelung.
Mag es Klarheit für ihn, Aufklärung, Bereicherung für
die Freunde, für Gleichfühlende bringen, Werbung oder
Verteidigung sein, es reinigt und entlastet ihn.

JACOB WASSERMAN in *Der Literat*

ON 19th January this year, the Society of the Friends of Music,
conducted by Oscar Fried, honoured me by devoting one of
their programmes exclusively to my compositions. For me, the
evening was important; the performance was brilliant, the
public attentive and receptive, and the subsequent criticism on
the whole conveyed much respect and goodwill, and was
agreed in the opinion that I want the New with emphasis on
the "want". I forestalled this reproach once already (but in
vain!) when I wrote the following sentence: "The creator
really only strives for perfection. And as he brings this into
harmony with his individuality a new law arises unintentionally."

The "new" is included in the idea of "Creation"—for in that
way creation is distinguished from imitation.

One follows a great example most faithfully if one does not
follow it, for it was through turning away from its predecessor
that the example became great.

* Written in Berlin, February 1912, for the periodical *Pan*.

46

It was in this sense that Arnold Schönberg spoke when, to a small community of people, he showed what little help can be got from the theory of composition, for it only teaches what is known. Creativeness, however, wants the unknown.

But the unknown is existent. The only question is, how to produce it.

There is no new and old. Only known and not yet known. Of these, it seems to me that the known still forms by far the smaller part.

A *Fantasia Contrappuntistica* was the first item on the programme of 19th January. This work grew out of the attempt to complete J. S. Bach's last unfinished fugue. It is a study. (Every self-portrait of Rembrandt's is a study; every work is a study for the next one; every life's work a study for those who come after.) The Bach fragment is planned on four fugue subjects, of which two are complete and the third commenced. The fragment breaks off when the three themes meet together for the first time, but the "development" of these three themes is lacking.

A fugue with three subjects is always a much dreaded task. The three subjects, however, were given, and the way in which they fitted together had been made clear and the themes are productive contrapuntally.

The fourth subject, on the other hand, had to be a completely new creation; there was no clue as to its character. There was the inevitable stipulation that this fourth subject had to sound simultaneously with the three earlier ones and must also suit them. As the principal theme of the *Art of Fugue* (of which the "Fragment" forms the close) was not one of the three subjects already worked out it was easy to guess that this principal theme should step in (as fourth) and thus close the circle of the whole work. Bernhard Ziehn, in Chicago, gave an affirmative and conclusive answer to my question on this point, and I was able to begin this part of my work on sure ground.

From Bach's intervals I built, on these four, yet a fifth

(distinctly contrasted) theme, so that my ship now moved over the difficult waters with five taut sails.

A five part counterpoint admits of 120 changes of position of the voices. Without including the possibilities of inversion, augmentation, diminution, and transposition. One single form of the Stretto alone, also admits of 120 new "inversions". To these time-honoured resources from the armoury of the school I added from my own store, the alteration of intervals, of the rhythm, and the variation of the theme. In this way the possibilities of combination became as vastly numerous as those of chess playing. With such a number of them, it was possible to continue this very important masterly score and to finish it.

Since early childhood I have played Bach and practised counterpoint. At that time it was a mania with me and at least one Fugato actually comes into every one of my youthful works. Now I found myself a contrapuntalist again although from a completely new standpoint. Nature's unbroken and hidden work had accomplished a great deal in me unconsciously, and I became aware of unexpected acquisitions, which had matured inwardly. One of the most valuable of these was the newly-found harmony that can arise through independent polyphony. Thus, I had many tools in hand for the making of a good technical building, but above all I felt as an artist; and for me the work of art is the final aim of all human endeavour. Science, the State, Religion and Philosophy all appear to me as works of art, and delight and stir me only as such.

Form, imagination and feeling are indispensable to the artist, they are the most precious of all things—those to which he offers sacrifice—the sacrifice of himself. These things I put into my work of completion and in that way it became my own. I believed I was acting in accordance with the spirit of Bach, when I placed the latest possibilities of our present-day art in the service of his plan—as the organic continuation of his art—as he himself brought the latest possibilities of the art of his time to expression.

The *Fantasia Contrappuntistica* is thought of neither for

pianoforte nor organ, nor orchestra. It is music. The sound-medium which imparts this music to the listener is of secondary importance.

The second item at this same concert was a *Berceuse élégiaque*. A cradle song sung for the dead mother. Written for a small selected orchestra of strings and wind instruments, harp and celeste. With this piece, which is now two years old, I succeeded for the first time in hitting upon my own sound idiom and in *dissolving the form into the feeling*. This made it all the more surprising to me to read of my work being taken for the art of the Frenchman Debussy. I want to correct this error firmly.

Debussy's art propels his personal and clearly defined feeling out of his own nature, into the outer world. I endeavour to draw upon the Infinite which surrounds mankind and to give it back in created form.

Debussy's art implies a limitation which strikes many letters out of the alphabet and follows the example of a scholastic poetic pastime, of writing poems in which the A's and R's are omitted. I strive for the enrichment, the enlargement, and the expansion of all means and forms of expression. Debussy's music interprets the most varied feelings and situations with similar sounding formulas; for every subject I have endeavoured to find different and suitable sounds. Debussy's tone pictures are parallel and homophonic; I wish mine to be polyphonic and "multi-versal". In Debussy's music we find the chord of the dominant ninth as a harmonic foundation and the whole tone as a melodic principle, without their merging together. I try to avoid every system, and to turn harmony and melody into indissoluble unity. He separates consonance and dissonance; I teach the denial of this difference. I "try", I "want", I "have endeavoured"—not that I have ever done it wholly or comprehensively, for I feel I am making a beginning whereas Debussy has reached an end.

The Concerto for Pianoforte, Orchestra and Men's Choir formed the third and last item on the programme. I endeavoured with this work to gather together the results of my

49

first period of manhood, and it represents the actual conclusion of it.

Like every work which falls into such a period of development, it is ripe through experience gained and supported by tradition.

It does not know about the future at all, but represents the present at the time of its origin. The proportions and the contrasts are carefully distributed and, in order that the plan should be firmly established before putting it into execution, nothing in it is accidental.

The old does not yield to the new but to the better. We have this advantage over the academicians in that we hope for the new whilst we honour the old; that we can suffer and enjoy at the same time; that we willingly humble ourselves without remaining inactive.

HOW I COMPOSE*

YOU ask in a questionnaire and yet in a way that seems to be addressed directly to me: How do people compose? I answer you willingly because it interests me to investigate the psychic mechanism. It can be said in a few words. First comes the idea, then the conception, or one seeks for it, then follows the execution. It is embarrassing to speak of oneself and it annoys others, yet I can only illustrate these scanty and vague theories with an example of my own. With your permission, therefore, I will choose one.

In the opera I am now working on, which is an opera and not a light opera, and is not called the *Braut-Wacht* nor the *Braut-Nacht*, but the *Brautwahl*, a change of scene occurs with a drop curtain between. The scene following shows a half-dark *Weinstube* in which an ancient mysterious Jew, Manasse, sits alone and silent. I used this intermission to paint with the orchestra a kind of portrait of this Hebrew. Old and surly, ghostlike and gruesome, rather a big, imposing person, and above all, an "Orthodox". "He seems to have come back from

* Answer to a questionnaire in the periodical *Der Konzertsaal*, Berlin, 1907.

a time long past", says E. T. A. Hoffmann, from whom I have borrowed the subject.

Do you see that now I have the idea? From this there is a hint that an extremely old Jewish melody could be used as a musical motive—it will certainly be familiar to you from synagogue ritual. Thus the interval of time between idea and conception was considerably shortened for me.

Now comes the execution. I wished this song, above all, to sound deep and gloomy. That determined the choice of instruments, and the right position for them determined the choice of the key.

In this way the execution advances further and builds itself up on Harmony, Characteristics, Form, Atmosphere, Colour and Contrast (with what precedes and what follows), and a hundred other details, until my Manasse stands there ready. So far I can certainly explain to you through sequence of thought how I compose. But through what suggestion the idea, the musical conception and the successful execution (which must also be fashioned out of many ideas) are hit upon, is a secret of inspiration, a thought which leads us out of the Jewish Orthodoxy into the sphere of Catholic mysticism. The origin of the idea can sometimes be referred to something seen, heard or read previously.

After all, every human work is only the elaboration of material existent on the earth. The musical invention and the first outline of execution come to me generally in the streets, in the evening, for preference, in a lively quarter. The execution proceeds at home in the free forenoons.

SELF-ASSESSMENT*

DURING the summer I examined my development and found that my progress had been great. As you know, I got beyond

* Extracts of letters to his wife—2nd August 1907, 8th November 1908, 23rd November 1904, 27th June 1908, 18th February 1911, 4th September 1905, 13th November 1919.

Schumann and Mendelssohn first of all in my musical taste. Liszt I misunderstood at first, then I adored him, and then quietly admired him. I was antagonistic to Wagner, then astonished by him, and then the Latin in me turned against him again. Berlioz amazed me; and I learnt to distinguish between good and bad Beethoven—which was one of the most difficult things to do. I discovered the newest French composers for myself and dropped them when they became popular too quickly. Finally my soul felt drawn towards the old Italian opera writers.

Those are the changes which have taken place over a period of twenty years, and all through those twenty years the score of *Figaro* has remained unchanged in my estimation, like a lighthouse in surging seas.

But when I looked at it again a week ago, I discovered human weakness in it for the first time; and my soul flew for joy when I realised that I am not so far behind it as I thought; in spite of this discovery being a real loss and pointing to the lack of durability in all human activities (and how much more in my own!) . . . .

I should like to catch hold of a corner of the coming art of music, and where possible, sew a seam in it myself—I feel more and more clearly that in the future all our present chirping will be defined as a "prehistoric" epoch. It can only be hoped that mankind, before it is too late, may turn away from this stupid urge towards quickness, excessive bigness, and possessions, so that great artists may still arise. It is a bad omen for the future that types should exist like R. S. who (even in his art) is a cross between an artist and an industrialist. And yet I almost think that in the new great music, machines will also be necessary and will be assigned a share in it. Perhaps industry, too, will bring forth her share in the artistic ascent.

As a human being and an artist I prefer to look forward rather than backward, and my preference for the company of younger people is connected with this fact. And I hope it will be like this until the end.

Digging into the past is repulsive to me.

My development as a composer would already be at quite a different stage if it had not been for the long interruptions and having to gather up the threads again so laboriously. I have only four months in the year in which to produce some better work and then I have to take a little step backwards again.

No, my existence as a composer really begins with the (Second) Violin Sonata.

Neither characterisation nor reproach can be of any help here. The case is as follows: as soon as I make my aim a *profitable* one, as soon as there begins to be a practical advantage in doing a thing, something in me begins to bleed, a kind of disablement overtakes me and it is only with pain and effort that I can carry through what, otherwise, I could achieve easily, happily and better. (You know that I *can* be industrious and energetic.)

A similar feeling comes over me when I see others behaving and thinking in a purely utilitarian manner in matters connected with art—and outside art too. . . .

If I am playing only because of the fee I always play badly, worse than the average pianist; besides this, I am always *ashamed* while I am playing and afterwards too, and that is distressing.

TWO AUTOBIOGRAPHICAL FRAGMENTS*

MY parents were both musicians and I was born on 1st April 1866 in Empoli, a little town close to Florence. My mother

* Part I was written in the years 1905–1908. Part II in February and March 1902, in Milan and Rome. Both were published for the first time in *Die Musik*, Year XXII, Vol. I.

was a much esteemed and—as far as I can judge—gifted pianist called Anna Weiss. On her father's side she was of German descent but on her mother's side Italian. My father is of pure Italian descent, the root of his genealogical tree, however, being in Corsica. Before my birth my mother played much in public, and with success, her last performance—eight days before my appearance—being in Rome, where she also played to Liszt in his house. My father was a clarinettist, he used his instrument in special ways as a soloist, sometimes emanating from the violin, sometimes from Italian song. His whole life long he scorned a post in an orchestra, half from pride and half because he was a natural artist, who worked things out more by instinct than by knowledge, and to whom reading from music and the division of bars presented some difficulties. My mother, on the other hand, was correctly trained and her playing belonged to the line of pianists coming from the Thalberg school; very fluent, somewhat in the salon style, and pianistic in the purest sense.

Already from my seventh year onwards my parents began to focus their entire interest on me and as artists they gradually worked less themselves. I played in public when I was seven and a half, and already when I was eight years old I played the C minor Concerto by Mozart very precisely and with fine details and a year later I gave concerts in Vienna, where I created some sensation.

II

AT the age of nearly forty-three and having arrived at a certain degree of maturity in the art, I see how others begin to interest themselves in my person with more sympathy than historical exactitude. To me, therefore, it seems fitting and not wasted effort that I myself should relate a little about my life. Should this report possess no other value, it will at least have the merit of being authentic.

I was baptised with the names Ferruccio Dante Michelangelo Benvenuto, and my father (without knowing it) followed the theory of old Shandy who assigned to the name an influence on the abilities of the bearer—a heavy responsibility which I lightened for myself by striking out the three great Tuscan artists and only keeping the name Ferruccio.

As a child, however, I signed myself Ferruccio Benvenuto and my father, always seeking easily-won fame, added to Busoni the family name of my mother who had acquired a good standing as a pianist.

At a certain period my father also enjoyed a little fame as clarinet player in several places; he thought his son was well cared for with those four resounding names and the magic exercised by the combination of Weiss-Busoni.

These Weiss-Busonis were engaged in full concert activity just before my birth—and only eight days before this event my mother made a public appearance in Rome where the public and the artists were honoured by the distinguished presence of Franz Liszt. The near prospect of the genealogical event made my father return to his birthplace Empoli where, surrounded by a host of relations and after really desperate difficulties, I saw the light of day. It was on Easter Sunday, the 1st April 1866.

Empoli, which lies between Florence and Pisa, is avoided by strangers and has therefore remained immaculate in its Tuscan culture. It first makes itself obtrusively perceptible by the smell from the vapours of its tanneries and match factories; to the eye, on the other hand (at least at the time of my birth), in a negative way through the lack of gas lighting.

Having remained chiefly commercial and industrial Empoli only offers a little evidence of Tuscan art. The Piazza shows the façade of a church "in the purest style" and without any upward swing. In front of it there is a fountain adorned with four marble lions, two of them, one is assured, are the work of a well-known artist; however it is generally left to the art student or the art lover to decide to which pair this precedence belongs. Somewhat outside the centre of the town lies the *Campaccio*, a very extensive unpaved square used as a horse market. And in one of the little houses that surround it I came into this world. Worthy of note in Empoli was the Festival of the Donkey's Flight which, until a few years ago, was celebrated on every Corpus Christi Day. This mocking ceremony was directed against the dwellers in Volterra, who had incautiously maintained that it would be just as easy for the people of Empoli to conquer them as for a donkey to fly. But the valiant ones of Empoli carried the day and also proved that a donkey could fly. The thought of this flying animal was quite easily conceived and carried out. A donkey was taken to the top of the bell-tower and from there it was let down on a rope. In order to increase the illusion still more, they fastened a pair of golden wings to it. So far as I know this appearance was the only example of a Pegasus of which Empoli could boast; for one knows of no poet from this town and the only name, up to the present, which is a little famous, remains that of a certain painter Jocopo. I know that when I was eight months old I was brought away from my native place and two years later I found myself in Paris with my parents. The rumour of war (which broke out in 1870) made my father, partly from caution, move from uncertain and dangerous ground; a decision which my father's nomadic nature favoured. So he began to play the clarinet again while wandering through Italy.

The uncertainty of this life (an uncertainty which for him continued unchanged from then on) and at that time the still good impulse to spare my mother the discomforts which belong to a life of adventure moved him to separate from his wife—I think for a period of two years. Meanwhile my mother and I were in Trieste where we made our abode in my grandfather's house, "Sor Giuseppe Weiss".

At this time my seventy-year-old grandfather lived in his spacious apartment (which stood nearly empty in consequence of the departure of his whole family) with his servant Mathilde as his mistress. This bad woman tyrannised over the whole house and understood how to put herself between my mother and my grandfather in such a way that the former suffered from it incessantly. And yet she was compelled to live with an infatuated father who, because he did not wish to allow the marriage, had shown her husband the door before their wedding. My mother, now returning to her father's house, was in no way able to prove the rightness of her choice; on the contrary, the whole lay-out of the thing was against her. She suffered from her husband's absence, the almost malicious indifference of her father, and from the excessive power of a low and vulgar woman, who took advantage of the circumstances to heap every kind of insult on my mother, showing no respect in her behaviour. She always behaved as complete mistress and increased more and more the misunderstanding between father and daughter. Until I began to form my own judgment I had a wrong conception of my grandfather. The impression at that time and my father's incessant slanders had completely distorted the true idea of the man for me.

My grandfather had an extremely strong character—it went as far as stubbornness—very upright and conscientious and gifted with many talents. When he was only thirteen his father had left him to his own devices and the boy had found a post as cabin boy on a ship going to the East. My grandfather therefore had only himself and his energetic and straightforward nature to thank for everything. In Trieste where he went ashore at a mature age, he succeeded with great efforts in obtaining a highly esteemed position for himself, he married a girl from one of the best families and kept himself without reproach in the esteem he had acquired until the age of ninety-three, when cheerfully, without illness or suffering, he came to the end of his life.

One evening, it must have been in the autumn of 1872, remains unforgettable. We still lived alone in Trieste, my mother and I, when she took me on that memorable evening to a *Teatro Meccanico* which, because of the topographical positions at that time, was to be found somewhat outside the town; at the crossing of the Via del Torrente and the Corsía del Stadion. In this theatre—it was much more like a barracks—scenes were performed, acted by puppets who moved by means of an inner mechanism without help from visible wires. One scene made a lively impression on me, namely when one of the figures drank a bottle of wine in such a way that one saw the contents get less and the liquid gradually pass into the puppet's mouth until the bottle was finally empty. After the performance we went quietly home, without fear and without hope, in that state of melancholic indifference which is frequently to be found in small Italian families; especially if something rather out of the common has been enjoyed and now one's thoughts turn again to everyday monotony.

We had gone about fifty steps when a *Signor* stood in our way. He was very imposing in appearance and wore a great beard divided into two points, something like a pair of top boots which reached to the knees. He led a very well-behaved, agreeable poodle on a steel chain, as if it were a wild animal; and the man's whole bearing was something like that of a master of the horse, or an animal tamer. My mother greeted him, a little moved and a little embarrassed. The gentleman embraced me and called me "Ferruccio" many times in a voice full of emotion and excitement. From these signs and from the recollection they awoke in me—kept alive through pictures and letters—I recognised my father. He had come back unexpectedly. It was to me as if this surprise should promise I know not what festivity. That smile between emotion and uncertainty froze on my mother's lips and I experienced a little storm in my heart that was an invisible but perhaps much stronger reflection of this smile.

My life changed completely after that evening.

My father at once took energetic measures whereby my

mother left the house of this "murderer of a father" as my father loved to express himself with regard to his father-in-law. Two rooms were taken in the Via Geppa, opposite the Turkish Consulate. The Consul's daughter—a child about eight or ten years—sometimes showed herself at the window which faced us, and it was there that I exchanged my first gallant glances. My father set to work as quickly as possible to instil the knowledge of piano-playing into me, for I had shown talent for this instrument when I was four, and I played by ear and performed with my mother certain little pieces by Diabelli for four hands. My father, who understood little about piano-playing and who was also uncertain about rhythm, made up for these deficiencies by a quite indescribable energy, strength and pedantry, so that he was able to remain seated beside me for four hours a day and to control every note and finger. There was no escape, no rest, and no imaginable lack of care on his side. The only pauses were brought about by the out-bursts from his prodigiously fiery temperament, which resulted in some boxes on the ear, copious tears, threats, dark prophecies and reproaches. All this ended finally in reconciliation, fatherly emotion and the assurance that he wished for nothing but my good—only to begin afresh in a few days' time. My father accomplished so much that barely a year later he was able to present me to the public; I think in the autumn of 1873, when I was seven and a half or almost eight years old. And after two more years he declared that I was developed and marvellous enough for him to take me to Vienna in the capacity of pianist, composer and extemporiser, protected by the shield of those names Ferruccio Benvenuto Weiss-Busoni. Neither did he forget to arm himself with his concert clarinet; he had scarcely sufficient means to come through and understood no word of German. We put up at the hotel for princes and famous people (Erzherzog Carl) and we were fortunate enough to meet Rubinstein, to whom my father found the opportunity of introducing me and insisted on my "playing for him". This "playing for him" still sounds dreadful in my ears. My father met no one in the street or in a coffee house without telling him about "his son"—the end of it was that he took the stranger home, rushed into the room, pulling the new acquaintance behind him and throwing the dreadful "play for him" in my face. This stranger was always a "distinguished personality" for my father until he got to know him better. The result of this nearer approach was that in my father's words he was "an imbecile", a "good-for-nothing", or something similar. Sometimes he succeeded in becoming an "excellent person" again (*una persona distintissima*) after he had conceded a modest loan of money. For the financial position was and always remained scanty under my father's administration however considerable the sums that went through his hands: because he invariably robbed Peter to pay Paul and never succeeded in finding a final remedy. I had to suffer from this condition during the whole of my childhood and youth, and for my father it has never ceased to be otherwise to this day.

THE *TURANDOT* MUSIC*

WITHOUT losing my way in the—to me—unfamiliar domain of literary criticism on the history of literature, I should like to make a few introductory remarks which apply solely to my music to Gozzi's *Turandot*, and how I regard the task I undertook.

In German musical literature there is a small number of classical models of music to the spoken drama. *Egmont* by Beethoven, *Manfred* by Schumann, *A Midsummer Night's Dream* by Mendelssohn, besides the exquisite half-opera *Oberon* by Weber.

In the literature of Italian music, on the other hand, nothing of this kind is known to me—and I may consider my music to Gozzi's *Turandot* as the first attempt to illustrate an Italian play with music.

Gozzi himself called for a great deal of music, and the

* Written in Berlin, October 1911, for the *Blätter des Deutschen Theaters*.

occasion for it is offered not only by the rhythms of marches and dances which demand it but still more by the fabulous character of the subject.

In fact a "fairy drama" without music is hardly thinkable and especially in *Turandot* where no magic is mixed up with it, and the grateful and needful rôle of representing what is supernatural and out-of-the-ordinary falls to the lot of the music. I have employed exclusively original oriental motives and forms and believe I have avoided the conventional theatre exoticism.

I had the original Italian text at hand, of course, as I composed my *Turandot*, without taking into consideration Schiller's adaptation: for I regard Schiller's work as an adaptation and not as a translation, and had I used it I should have had the feeling of alienating myself from the spirit of Gozzi. For me, the essential thing in the original text was the feeling—even in the scenes bordering on the tragic—of always being concerned with a matter of fantasy. Schiller throughout fails to convey this. The masked figures, familiar to Italians, contribute to this effect excellently, for they throw a bridge from the Venetian public into the fictitious Orient of the stage and in this way destroy the illusion that what is going on is real life.

This rôle of bridge-maker falls to the lot of the Pantaloon especially, for he is the personification of Venetian wit and continually recalls the actual place by the allusions he makes to his native town and by using turns of speech belonging to the dialect of that district. It was this continuous gaily-coloured change of passion and make-believe, of reality and unreality, of the commonplace and the fantastically exotic, which charmed me most in Gozzi's *Chinese Fairy Tale for the Theatre*.

ARLECCHINO'S EVOLUTION*

THE sketch for the libretto of *Arlecchino* originated in the spring of 1914 when there was still no war to fear. This sketch,

* Written in Rome, April 1921, for the *Blätter der Staatsoper Berlin*, Vol. VII.

which was then locked up temporarily, was decisive, on the whole, for the later version (October 1914). The slaughter which had broken out in between was the cause of the original "Turks" of the libretto being changed into "Barbarians". One character was struck out of the first *dramatis personae*. She was drawn as an ageing prima donna who angled for the knight and spied out from her window. The development of a situation thus brought about gave occasion for an upbraiding duet between her and Colombina. This person was taken out of the cast as not being essential to the philosophy of the piece; thereby the circle of the scenes could be drawn round a purer symbol. There were still some musical sketches which would have taken until Christmas to commit to paper: the overture, the praise of wine, the theme for the quartet, and the "Italian Revenge" Aria (which was the first and foremost inspiration). At this point, because of my departure from Berlin, the composition was seriously interrupted and it was only taken up again and finished in the peace of my Swiss sojourn towards the end of 1915. It was accepted for performance by the Zürich Stadttheater, but the theatre director and I were at a loss for a work which would have to be given with *Arlecchino* in order to fill the evening bill for the theatre. The unsolved question made me decide to contribute a second piece myself. Three months later, therefore, the text and score of *Turandot* were ready, so that the first performance of both operas took place during the same season.

I got the idea for *Arlecchino* from the masterly performance of an Italian actor (Piccello, if I remember rightly) who tried to re-introduce the old *commedia dell'arte*, and in it he spoke and played the rôle of my hero surpassingly well. At the same time I got to know the Roman marionette theatre and their performance of the little comic opera written by Rossini when he was twenty (*The Travelling Bag or Opportunity Makes the Thief*) left a deep impression on me. My *Theatralisches Capriccio* arose out of these two experiences. The first of them exercised an appreciable influence on the poetry, the second on the composition. The ideal place in which to set the scene was Bergamo, which is Arlecchino's native place and which, like every Italian provincial city, has its own masked figure that represents the wit of the people. *Arlecchino* is a dramatised confession and therefore entirely my own work apart from the stimulus I have mentioned. It is at one and the same time a light mockery of life and of the theatre; of most sincere intent, with all its unpretentiousness and comedy meant seriously, and undertaken with the most loving care for the artistic form.

This endeavour demanded some changes in the libretto during the course of transposing it into sound. Isolated sentences, not inappropriate as words, in places disturbed the musical form.

Some of the places which were suppressed I will put down here. For example, just at the beginning it ran as follows:

MATTEO

"Galeotto fu'l libro e chi lo scrisse. . . ."

He breaks off

It transpires that a certain Galeotto has been the go-between between Lanzelot and Ginevra.

. . . Symbols ah Symbols!

And so on. Later:

ABBATA

The gallant master tailor's beautiful wife lives here,
A little light green tree
Who stretches out her little twigs towards the sun
Out of the crevices in the cracked masonry—

DOTTORE

—And winks at lovers!

63

ABBATA

Indulgence, indulgence, Doctor Bombasto.
Be satisfied with killing sick bodies
And let young healthy shoots live. . . .

And so on. At the beginning of the trio the following was
added:

MATTEO

Do you know nothing of it?

ABBATA

I know something anyhow,
The Barbarians or Germans
Are the people of music and philosophy
Although in the one they do not reach
To our sublime Alessandro Scarlatti
Nor in the other to my god-like Plato.

MATTEO

. . . They surround this town. . . .

And so on. In the dialogue between Arlecchino and Colombina, Arlecchino expressed himself at greater length and to the
renouncement of fidelity this was also added:

ARLECCHINO

How is your sleep, Madam?

COLOMBINA

My sleep is uneasy
Because I grieve about you!

ARLECCHINO

That is bad for the complexion.

64

COLOMBINA

Do I really look so bad?

ARLECCHINO

Make your mind easy you look very charming.
Still, do your dreams evolve round me alone?
Are you certain? There is also a secret infidelity
Which leaves worse traces because it does not act
And truly stinks like stagnant waters—
Impotent infidelity! I speak in general.

COLOMBINA

You talk horribly. . . .

And so on. Colombina's seductive conversation was more
copious in words. She said:

I dance, play the tambourine and sing,
Prepare your favourite dishes in a savoury manner,
Embroider scrolls on your handkerchief (always more
softly and catlike),
And arm-in-arm we go out of doors,
Visit the church at mid-day,
Later in the evening our dear friends,
And in the evening to the theatre,
Where we laugh or cry together
Whatever the piece brings [*gently*]
Then comes the night.

ARLECCHINO

[*To himself*]   Put a good quarrel there. . . .

All these and many less important points were sacrificed to
the musical form which goes hand-in-hand with the theatrical

form in a play which is sung. This stratagem of renunciation is one of the artist's virtues in the case of all broadly laid out plans. There is this compensation that in other places the inspiration demands equally irresistibly unforeseen amplifications and interpolates unplanned material. This happened to *Arlecchino* too, for as a poem it experienced (subsequently) a detailed completion.

Der Arlecchineide Fortsetzung und Ende spins the ethical idea of the piece further, outwardly separate from the operatic work, scarcely fit for music, and hardly performable; a more abstract *fantasie*. It will shortly appear as a book.

THE MEANING OF *ARLECCHINO* *

ABOVE all it did me good to read that you have been moved by my little theatre piece. The understanding of one single friend amply atones for the misunderstanding of the majority of people. I have been reproached for *Arlecchino* because it is considered scornful and inhuman: nevertheless, this creation arose from an impulse completely opposed to such feelings—namely, out of sympathy for men who make life harder for one another than it should and might be, through egoism, through inveterate prejudices, and through convention when it is opposed to feeling! Therefore, in *Arlecchino* one comes (and this aim is attained) only to a painful laugh. Even the knight, who is the most harmless character, is drawn with irony, at times with a touch of bitterness.

The title rôle gives my own confessions. The Abbé expresses human forbearance and tolerance. The tailor Matteo is the duped idealist, suspicious of nothing. Colombina—the woman. After that of *The Magic Flute* (which I value highly) it is the most moral libretto there is.

* From a letter to Margarete Klinckerfuss, written on 19th May 1918 and published in her book, *Aufklänge aus versunkener Zeit* (Port Verlag—Urach, 1947).

APROPOS OF *ARLECCHINO**

POLICE PREFECT: The fact is, we have all been a good deal puzzled because the affair *is* so simple, and yet baffles us altogether.

DUPIN: Perhaps it is the very simplicity of the thing which puts you at fault.

POLICE PREFECT: (laughing heartily) What nonsense you *do* talk.

DUPIN: Perhaps the mystery is a little *too* plain.

POLICE PREFECT: Good heavens, who ever heard of such an idea?

DUPIN: A little *too* self-evident.

POLICE PREFECT: (roaring with laughter) Ha! ha! ho! ho! Dupin, you will be the death of me yet.

E. A. POE, *The Purloined Letter*

From Mozart I learnt to say important things in a conversational way.

BERNARD SHAW whilst conversing with F. Busoni

THERE is nothing dangerous in flinging risky or just clever hypotheses into the intellectual world, but it certainly is dangerous when they are brought forward as conclusive principles. The maker of hypotheses who is conscious of what can be seen still further and apprehended still more, is prone to make this error less frequently, just because he does see further and apprehend more. But his partisans all the more certainly fall into the error and—from the auto-mechanism of reaction— his opponents also. Both distort the sense of the original idea; the one out of blind belief, the other from the instinct of contradiction. And an idea of failure is left, which is the case with everything that has been through too many hands and opinions. Amongst these, hands which are unavoidably awkward and opinions which are without understanding effectively destroy

* Berlin, May 1922.

the first thought—not always from a bad intention. The hypothesis has originated in one brain and it is cut to the measure of that brain and is fundamentally *personal*. At times the joy of having made the discovery misleads the discoverer himself into generalising his idea, and he sees and values it as applicable universally; whilst really, first and foremost, it is part and parcel of the special brain that produced it and usually stands and falls with that brain.

If the originator of the hypothesis is unprejudiced and clear-sighted enough to limit the range of his creation, others make a point of giving it a meaning and an application beyond its sphere. Only a platitude remains incontestable and the more comprehensive a truth is, the more like a platitude it sounds.

The smaller minds who would very much like to have a share in it wish to look behind it for more than it contains, and are busily at work with interpretation and amplification. The opponents, no less, in their zeal to disclaim and destroy, often lend weight to the worn-out truism, just through the power of negation.

Arlecchino is less than a challenge and more than a jest.

To feel it as a challenge is putting it at a disadvantage, and to represent it as something not to be taken seriously is to belittle it. In the end it stands almost "jenseits von Gut und Böse"—"beyond Good and Evil"—(with an inclination towards the good). And finally, it is an independent work of art.

Its incidental content of confession and instruction is not important enough to cross the path of what is artistic or to turn it away from that path. As a work of art it is sufficiently aristocratic to be able to claim a line of ancestors which makes it legitimate. As a handicraft it belongs to the scores that are made carefully and fastidiously. Is it pleasing? Has it significance? It endeavours to unite both excellences in the way proposed by the director of the theatre in the prologue to *Faust*.

At least it is pleasing in the lightness of the action and anyhow significant in the sense that it hides a meaning in itself, and consequently signifies something. On the other hand, it has a tendency to ambiguity and hyperbole in order to place the listener, momentarily, in a position of slight doubt; it adheres consciously to the constant play of colour between grim jest and playful seriousness, and this is carried on throughout.

Here are the incidents contained in this piece, put concisely:

Deceived husband, unaware of his own fate, mounts a hobby-horse which does not help him on; with his house shaking under his feet he bars it firmly outside and leaves the inside free.

★   ★   ★

There come to him his friends, a doctor and a priest, honest bunglers of the body and soul; the two figures are swallowed by the door of an inn; they argue energetically to avoid action.

★   ★   ★

And again there is a threat of war, alarm of the burghers; it is the barbarians who shake the peace, men get up quickly and seize sticks, and even the sheep are wakened by the shouting.

★   ★   ★

But gallantry, coxcombry, lyrical dalliance and the old-inherited darkness are of service to the wife, who with subtle charm, follows the second and gives the first the slip.

★   ★   ★

There is a challenge to a duel together with sharp words; the mere spectacle draws the curiosity of the people, but they will not be disturbed in their laziness for this, and retire to their homes and shut the shutters.

★   ★   ★

The donkey proves as helpful as ever, dragging after him the cart filled with such gay colours. How unselfish, poor in fame, rich in peace he is; some of the splendour of heaven falls upon him.

★   ★   ★

I had almost forgotten the hero of the title, his dress is

69

motley and his nature bold, he loves, he fights, and laughs, he flies and sings and is like one possessed with the devil of truth.

THE SCORE OF *DOKTOR FAUST**

IT was my wish and principle to make the central point of my opera a figure conspicuous and proverbial in history, connected with magic and unsolved riddles. From Zoroaster to Cagliostro these figures form a row of pillars through the course of time, and in this case the figure to be chosen from among them should not be so far in the past as to cause suffering to the participator because of the distance, nor so far forward that the indispensable "distance" would be too short for the effect. I decided therefore on that part of the Middle Ages beginning to be lighted up by the dawn of the Renaissance.

In 1911, in Paris, I discussed with d'Annunzio, in detail, a libretto about Leonardo da Vinci, the "Italian Faust" as the poet called him, and moreover the poet objected, "A skeleton with a torch put in the place of a head." In him the poet missed the indispensable material for the "lyric" which he could not do without, owing to his conception of opera taken over from the nineteenth century, and because he was an Italian and an apostle of Wagner. This is the reason for his speaking of the "fleshless, heartless skeleton", the "merciless clarifying light it carries in place of a head".

Merlin interested me transitorily; Don Juan for a longer time but here I was obliged to retire before Mozart's great model—even if it had been possible to lay hands on quite a different Don Juan libretto from that of the skilful Abbate da Ponte. Monks would have to take part in it, movements in the underworld, and the Holy Inquisition. Moors, Believers, and Jews. Trained singers and virtuosi who could perform the madrigals in the best possible way. The suppression of the stone-guest's counter-invitation, acted in a ruined chapel,

* See note on p. 1.

seems to me an outstanding opportunity missed. An extremely impressive example of this is to be found in *El Burlador de Sevilla* by Tirso de Molina, under which name the fictitious monk, Gabriel Tellez, concealed his identity. Here, too, a powerful figure of a fisherwoman appears who surpasses all the figures of women in the later Don Juan romances.

The intention and still more the desire to provide Goethe's *Faust* with music has deeply engrossed me, but veneration for the overpowering task led me to renounce it. This confession, I think, emerges clearly out of the rhymed prologue. To recognise one's own limit, and to admit it, leads one nearest to the right use of inborn capabilities. But I had fallen under the fascination of the Faust idea, and continued to be ruled by it. I was freed from the swaying dissention between longing and renunciation by my ensuing acquaintance with the old puppet-show, of which I inspected several versions, for *that*, I decided, would be the starting-point of the libretto of my opera.

In six days, as if in a fever, I wrote down the first sketch for *Doktor Faust*; between the outbreak of war and the preparation for a sea voyage, towards the end of 1914.

My own drama begins with the scene at the court of Parma and steps therewith out of the mystical into the worldly. From instinct Faust aspires to union with the Duchess, not yet being conscious of the final aim himself. A reminder of the final aim is the transmission of the dead child, with Mephistopheles as courier. But still Faust does not grasp the importance of the reminder and Mephistopheles misleads him still further by making him believe, through trickery, that the living Ideal would come forth from the dead child. This proves to be a fallacy incapable of fulfilment, and Faust renounces the attainment of the Ideal, as he has already renounced the resources of magic (this emerges out of the ensuing conversation with the students' shadows).

In the last picture the vision of the Duchess makes it forcibly clear to Faust what the child signifies to him. After Faust, in his last attempt at an approach to God, has also thrown away belief, he proceeds to mystical deeds which renew his exhausted life.

For reasons which I have explained in the first part of the preface, there are intentional gaps in the libretto and it is apparently fragmentary. In this way space is left free to be filled out by the music, while there are enough situations and catch-phrases to make a basis. On the other hand the act with the exorcism became a little diffuse; the wish to give orders to the Devil is no light undertaking.

I hope that Faust's fear can be discerned, the fear that makes him collapse unconscious at the end. After all, he goes to the shelter of the magic circle (to oppose the evil formulas, the exorcist's belt being used for this) with a drawn sword, and this he keeps in his right hand.

This is a symbol, showing that the exorcist remains armed against danger. The whole transaction is considered extremely dangerous in the art of magic. It should be noticed that after he becomes aware of the fifth voice, the disillusioned Faust steps out of the circle and by doing so ceases to be invulnerable.

Thereupon, although unasked, the sixth voice announces itself, and Faust is unable to defend himself against it any longer. For good reasons I have struck out the first monologue of the puppet play (which Goethe takes over almost literally) for to begin the piece in such a way would have been too reminiscent of the conventional *Faust* and the onlooker would be tuned to expect similar familiar pictures. In addition to this, the sense of the monologue is contained in Mephistopheles' threat later on, when he puts Faust's desperate situation in front of his eyes. Consequently, with me the play begins with the introduction of the students. In the puppet play they are only mentioned, but here they come into the vision in action and their number is changed from the original two to the mystical three.

Already, before writing the libretto, I had consciously made musical studies for *Faust* in my *Nocturne Symphonique* and my *Sonatina Seconda*. The themes and style of these pieces were used in the score and happily fulfilled the task prepared for them with regard to stimulation, compass, and atmosphere. In the middle of the whole work, separated and yet dependent, I composed, half experimentally, a *Sarabande* and *Cortège* (a model reduced in size). Hearing these performed gave me further certainty and instruction.

Before anything else it was necessary to sketch out the complete plan, the larger outlines of which were previously indicated by the words, to think over the choice, distribution, and employment of means and forms (forms in time and in movement). The principal thing for me to do was to mould musically independent forms which at the same time suited the words and the scenic events and which also had a separate and sensible existence detached from the words and the situation. Just as melody stands above all the means there are for composition, so, as a means of sound, the human voice remains the most important and richest in expression; the most living instrument and the one most full of soul, which stands out triumphantly from the other artificial instruments, carrying further than the others, penetratingly audible out of doors and at a distance (it is not out of place to repeat the commonplace knowledge here). On the other hand, the limitations of this, the noblest of all means of sound, arise from the dependence on speech (for emphasis) and text (for train of thought), the shortness of breath, the restricted compass, and the lack of precision which easily appears.

Against this, the expression of one of the simplest of phrases can be effectively intensified by the singing voice, increasing the expressiveness surprisingly. Listen to the following simple melody of Mozart's which appears in one of his piano concertos:

Ex.2

then listen to it sung (perhaps to these words):

Ex.3

See how the exuberant interval of a sixth now first attains its complete importance, how the repetition of the half-bar figures make an impressive effect through the repetition of the words in unison with them; how from the clavecin motive an almost passionate sentence arises, the interpolated sense of the words lending life to the intervals—that is the magic of the human voice.

The melodic element has yet another significance in instrumentation; it is helpful, ennobling, and it carries the content; indeed it is indispensable. That is why it seems to me that the development inside the musical·structure strives to put an orchestral movement together out of the pure melodic lines, which cross and support each other and move independently, and from which the harmony arises. In the score of *Doktor Faust* I have adhered almost throughout to these polyphonic lines and restricted the harmonic formation, the graphic picture of the notes being more horizontal than vertical. This is one of the characteristic points of the score that has to be mentioned. Here is another. It has always been a cause of dissatisfaction to me (certainly without accounting for the first impression) that the acting space for a play ends with the terminating line of the painted scene and thus is cut off from the onlooker.

To him half of the circle in which the action takes place always remains hidden (as happens to the moon in relationship to the earth). Yet, in thought, the organic expanse of the circle is not dismissed, and in the play there are plenty of indications to show that the transactions continue spinning their threads behind the view. The onlooker's imagination is asked to work at the completion. If a figure goes out of a door, the departure gives the onlooker a vivid picture of the person going out into the street.

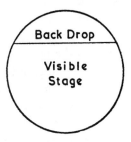

At times, too, he knows where the person is going (imagined) and thus he fathoms the invisible half of the circle with the eye of imagination.

It is different with music in the theatre which (except in the fewest cases) fills out the front half of the circle exclusively. To me it is precisely music that is qualified to encircle this circumference and in this score I have made the first attempt (not completely carried out) to create an horizon of sound, an acoustic perspective, in which I frequently allow what is sung and acted behind the scenes to sound; in this way the unseen will be revealed by the hearing. This is the second point to be mentioned. A third: some time ago I wrote to a friend, "Inspiration is gift, opinion a thing of character, but it is form that first makes the owner of these two attributes into an artist." I have always and with the greatest exactitude taken pains over form. How I apply it and practise it in the foregoing case can be shown by some examples.

The six voices of the demon, in the second Overture, I gathered into a row of variations, arranged on the question and answer motive. At the same time I purposed taking these voices gradually from the deep to the higher register (mounting singly) from dragging slowness to increasing movement, so that the last voice is the highest and therefore the rôle of Mephistopheles must be sung by a definite tenor.

The scenic intermezzo—which is acted in the "very ancient Roman chapel"—I succeeded in putting into the individual form of the Rondo, in spite of the events and moods in it, which follow one another so quickly. I set the garden festival at Parma to a Ballet Suite, acted in a kind of dumb-show; this is only replaced by freer dramatic gesture towards the end.

I devoted special study to the peal of bells that I used on three "occasions". At the beginning, in the orchestra, as a faint imitation, a shadowy recollection of swings in the distance, already dying away; as the dying away of the Symphonia, so that on the word "Peace" (Note: this portion was composed in 1917) it is taken over by human voices; and finally, at the end of the Overture, as a rejoicing from real church bells loudly proclaiming the resurrection.

Some verses which are thought of as Epilogue to the whole work, as *cul de lampe final*, will receive the place assigned to them here—anticipating and sealing.

The poet speaks to the onlooker:

> A history of man and his desire
> This night to sound of music has been told
> The tragedy of Faustus did inspire
> The tale of doom before your eyes unroll'd.
> So many metals cast into the fire,
> Does my alloy contain sufficient gold?
> If so, then seek it out for your own hoard;
> The Poet's travail is his sole reward.

> Still unexhausted all the symbols wait
> That in this work are hidden and conceal'd;
> Their germs a later school shall procreate
> Whose fruits to those unborn shall be reveal'd.
> Let each take what he finds appropriate;
> The seed is sown others may reap the field.
> So, rising on the shoulders of the past,
> The soul of man shall reach his heaven at last.

REMARKS ABOUT THE PROPER ORDER OF THE OPUS NUMBERS
OF MY WORKS*

AS a child I wrote much and published many things prematurely. Badly advised and inexperienced, I numbered the things which were printed according to the order of their origin instead of according to the sequence of their publication. So the little volume 30–40 was printed with this numbering although those marked 15–29 (21 and 25 excepted), were not yet printed. When I was about seventeen years old, op. 1–14 and 30–40 among the small compositions had fortunately been published.

At this time—when eighteen years old—the real youthful experiments arose and I began to consider systematising the numbers. At that time Albert Gutmann in Vienna published two songs op. 15, six studies op. 16, and another study in variation form op. 17. The last two were dedicated to Johannes Brahms.

My work took a serious turn after my journey to Leipzig in 1885 and this was followed in the autumn of 1887 by my flight from there in order to get away from troubled and unsettled home conditions. With my next work published by Kistner, I made up my mind to fill out the missing opus numbers in the printed sequence. I finished op. 18 and soon completed filling out the other numbers (1890). When I compared op. 30, the work of childhood which bears the number 30, with its successors, I saw the gap which had arisen in the meantime through my development. I could consent no longer to let those "thirties" pass as the continuation of the riper "twenties". I saw that the way out was to compose a new series of "thirties" to which for the sake of distinction I affixed the letter "A". Only the youthful work 37 (twenty-four Preludes), and 40 (four

* Sketched in Altenburg, 30th March 1908, and revised in Berlin, 25th April 1908. Published as a guide to the catalogue of works in the first edition of the publication.

Italian choruses for men with orchestral accompaniment) seemed to me to be of enough value not to require the substitution and in op. 39 instead of the letter "A" I chose the representation of the number in roman figures in the new series. The chronological sequence is thus:

1–14, 21, 25, 61, 70, 30–40	Childhood
15, 16, 17, 18, 19, 20, 22, 23, 24,	
25 (for the second time), 26, 27, 28, 29	} Youth
30a, 31a, 32a, 33a, 33b, 34a, 35a,	
36a, 38 (for the second time),	} Manhood up to 1906
xxxix, 41	

The Elegies should have been 42 but have appeared without an opus number, likewise *Kultaselle* (Variations for Violin).

In the ideal sense I first found my way as composer in the Second Violin Sonata (op. 36a), which among friends I also call my opus one, which (as real second and third) the Concerto and *Turandot* followed. But my entire personal vision I put down at last and for the first time in the Elegies (finished January 1908). By my seventeenth year I had composed a Rural Cantata in the compass of 300 pages of score which was performed successfully in the Teatro Communale at Bologna. From this work Arrigo Boito formed the most brilliant hopes for my prospects in the future as a composer, and when a few days ago on 12th April 1908 I saw this Master again for the first time since our meeting in Milan, he greeted me half reproachfully and said that I ought to have thought of nothing else but composition after that work at the age of seventeen. The Cantata remained unprinted.

Between 1887 and 1889 I completed sketches for the score of a romantic opera *Sigune or the Quiet Village*, which I did not work out; two concert pieces for piano and orchestra and a piano sonata have, with many small things, likewise remained unprinted.

IV

PIANO PLAYING AND PIANO MUSIC

THE PIANOFORTE SHOULD BE ESTEEMED*

ITS disadvantages are obvious, great and irremediable: the impossibility of sustaining the sound, and the pitiless, sharp division of the keyboard into unalterable half-tones. But its excellencies and prerogatives are little miracles.

With it a single person can command a complete whole: and it surpasses all other instruments by producing the softest and the loudest sound in one single register. Trumpets can blare and not murmur, flutes the reverse. The pianoforte can do both. It admits of the highest and lowest available sounds. The pianoforte should be esteemed. Let the doubter bear in mind how Bach, Mozart, Beethoven, esteemed the keyboard and dedicated to it their choicest thoughts.

And the pianoforte has one possession which is wholly peculiar to itself, an inimitable device, a picture of the sky, a ray of moonlight—the pedal. The potential effects of the pedals are still unexhausted because they have remained the slave of a narrow-minded and senseless harmonic theory; the way in which they are used is like trying to convey the movements of air and water by geometrical forms. Beethoven, who indisputably took the biggest stride in the development of the pianoforte, divined the nature of the pedal and we have to thank him for the first subtleties.

The pedal is decried. Senseless irregularities are to blame for this. Let us experiment with sensible irregularities. . . .

* Written in Berlin in the spring of 1910 for *Galston's Studienbuch*. The essay about the *Galston's Studienbuch* is not included in this edition.

THE REQUIREMENTS NECESSARY FOR A PIANIST*

NO, technique is not and never will be the Alpha and Omega of pianoforte playing any more than it is with any other art. Nevertheless, I certainly preach to my pupils: provide yourselves with technique and thoroughly too. Various conditions must be fulfilled in order to make a great artist, and it is because so few are able to fulfil them that a true genius is such a rarity.

Technique, perfect in and for itself, may be found in any well-constructed pianola. Nevertheless a great pianist must first of all be a great technician; but technique, which constitutes only a part of the art of the pianist, does not lie merely in fingers and wrists or in strength and endurance. Technique in the truer sense has its seat in the brain, and it is composed of geometry—an estimation of distance—and wise co-ordination. Even that, however, is only a beginning, for touch also belongs to true technique as does very particularly the use of the pedals.

Further, the great artist must necessarily have an unusual intelligence and culture. He must be widely educated in music and literature and in all matters affecting human existence. The artist must also have character. If one of these requisites is missing, the deficiency will be apparent in every phrase he plays. Then add to this feeling, temperament, imagination, poetry, and finally that personal magnetism which sometimes enables the artist to inspire four thousand people, strangers, whom chance has brought together, with one and the same state of feeling. There is still presence of mind which is also to be desired, control over moods in irritating conditions, the ability to rouse the attention of the public and finally in "psychological moments" to forget the public.

Shall one add the feeling for form and style, and the virtue of good taste and originality? How could one ever enumerate

* Written in Minneapolis at the beginning of 1910 for the *Signale der Musikalischen Welt*, Berlin.

all the qualities required? But one requirement comes before all others: *Anyone who will master the language of art must have nurtured his life through the soul.*

RULES FOR PRACTISING THE PIANO*

1. Practise the passage with the most difficult fingering; when you have mastered that, play it with the easiest.
2. If a passage offers some particular technical difficulty, go through all similar passages you can remember in other pieces; in this way you will bring system into the kind of playing in question.
3. Always combine technical practice with the study of the interpretation; the difficulty, often, does not lie in the notes but in the dynamic shading prescribed.
4. Never be carried away by temperament, for that dissipates strength and where it occurs there will always be a blemish, like a dirty spot which can never be washed out of a material.
5. Don't set your mind on overcoming the difficulties in pieces which have been unsuccessful because you have previously practised them badly; it is generally a useless task. But if meanwhile you have quite changed your way of playing, then begin the study of the old piece from the beginning as if you did not know it.
6. Study everything as if there were nothing more difficult; try to interpret studies for the young from the standpoint of the virtuoso. You will be astonished to find how difficult it is to play a Czerny or Cramer or even a Clementi.
7. Bach is the foundation of piano playing, Liszt the summit. The two make Beethoven possible.
8. Take it for granted from the beginning that everything is possible on the piano, even where it seems impossible to you and even when it really is so.

* From a letter to his wife, 20th July 1898.

9. Attend to your technical equipment so that you are prepared
and armed for every possible event; then when you study
a new piece, you can turn all your power on to the intellectual content; you will not be held up by the technical
problems.

10. Never play carelessly, even when there is nobody listening,
or the occasion seems unimportant.

11. Never leave a passage which has been unsuccessful without
repeating it; if you cannot do it immediately because of
the presence of others then do it subsequently.

12. If possible allow no day to pass without touching your
piano.

... What do you think of these "Maxims for Practice?"
They are formed from my own experience.

THE PIANOFORTE GENIUS*

DURING these first days of the century following that of
Liszt's birth, I have read the words "Pianoforte Genius" a
number of times in Berlin criticisms. Even little girls have had
it hung around their necks and were almost stifled, for as a
word genius is a heavy burden; the genius dies of his victories.
It is undeniable that there are today a great number of brilliant
and masterly pianists who can imitate everything which the
true pianoforte genius has invented, and do it so well that the
imitation is deceptive. In the Berlin papers, during the same
short space of time, it was asserted of five different pianists that
"one had never before heard the Liszt Sonata played so well".
I am convinced that all those performances were splendid, but
conclude therefrom that the execution of the Sonata by Liszt
is a problem which has been solved, and that this stage of

* Written in Berlin, March 1912, for the *Allgemeine Musik-Zeitung*.

pianoforte playing has become a general acquisition. Today anyone who is a pianist by vocation plays this piece well and accurately at eighteen. Instances of this, however (which I often meet with), cannot any longer be regarded as unusual but they illustrate the workings of atavism. Pianists of the present generation are born with the technique and style of this composition of Liszt's in their blood.

Similar phenomena may be observed in the realm of technology, especially among electrical engineers.

I know the sons of some quite simple people, still children in years, who, quite as a matter of course, carry out small tasks to do with electrical wiring in the house and look upon this as a pastime. Where do these talents come from, in a youth who is only averagely gifted, talents which 200 years ago could only have been produced by a "genius", a dare-devil, a magician? The answer obviously lies in inheritance and in the atmosphere of the times. Genius for the pianoforte should be—like genius in general—a gift which takes a new road and accomplishes unprecedented things: things which it takes others a little time to learn.

Such pianoforte geniuses were Beethoven, Chopin, and Liszt; they perceived new means, solved the problems of new effects, created "improbable difficulties" and wrote a literature of their own.

It can be asserted confidently that in this sense nothing has been added by even the most celebrated living pianists. It is indeed a very astonishing fact (at first glance!) that other people have the power to do that which only one could do formerly, but as soon as a whole multitude of "others" are existent it becomes Darwinism. He who stands alone when he appears in public and is only imitated later on by others, who compels pianoforte builders to consider new principles and creates a new literature in which experienced pianists do not find their way at once, has a lawful right to the title "pianoforte genius".

But then it is not conferred on him.

PLAYING FROM MEMORY*

Berlin, May 1907

Dear Professor,

Your interesting question "Should artists play from memory?" falls late into my hands on my return after a long absence. At your express invitation ("for some . . . letters from artists I should be much obliged") I take the liberty of writing to you. I, an old public performer, have reached the conclusion that playing by heart allows an incomparably greater freedom in performance.

For precision in playing it is important that the eyes (where it is necessary) can work unhindered at the keyboard. Moreover the dependence on someone to turn over is also a constraint, often a hindrance.

Besides which, one must in any case know the piece from memory in case one should lose the right line at the performance.

Further—and every advanced pianist will confirm this—a composition of some importance is impressed on the memory more quickly than into the fingers or the mind. There are very few exceptions. At the moment I can only think of the fugue from Beethoven's Sonata op. 106.

Stage fright, of course, to which everyone is liable more or less, occasionally—or frequently—affects the reliability of the memory, but release from relying on the memory does not, as you assume, affect stage fright. If stage fright appears the head becomes clouded and the memory falters, but if one uses music, stage fright will immediately appear in another form. Note inaccuracy, lack of rhythm, increase of speed. You complain that there are artists "who hawk around half a dozen concertos their whole life long" and, indirectly, you attribute this to playing from memory.

But Herr R. Pugno, whom you quote as a good example of playing from music, has no more piano concertos in his repertory.

* Answer to a questionnaire for *Die Musik*, Berlin, May 1907.

If I may be allowed to give you an explanation, it happens as follows: there are artists who study the instrument and the musical apparatus as a whole and artists who single out separate passages and separate pieces in order to make them their own.

To the latter every piece is a new problem to be solved again, laboriously from the beginning. They are obliged to construct a new key to every lock. The first named are locksmiths who, with a bundle of small picklocks and skeleton keys, can examine and overcome the difficulties of any lock. This refers to the technique as well as to the musical content and to the memory. If, for example, one has the key to Liszt's technique for passage work, to his melodic and harmonic system, to his formal structure (where does the accent lie, where the climax?) and to his style in expression of feeling, it is all the same whether one plays three or thirty of his pieces. I believe I have proved that this is no mere high-flown phrase.

The new task for the memory arises—in proportion—when one is concerned with a composer, a nation, an epoch, or a direction for which one has not yet constructed a general key. This happened to me the first time I tried César Franck.

I have come to the conclusion, therefore, that to anyone who has the vocation to play in public, memory is as little of a hindrance as, for example, the audience itself. But whoever makes a barrier out of playing from memory will also be a hesitator in everything else. The first mentioned plays the literature written for the instrument and the second chooses some pieces from it to let himself be heard. By this, the question is given quite another turn, namely: at what point does one have the right to play in public?

VALUE OF THE TRANSCRIPTION*

RATHER more than seventeen years ago when my impulse of enthusiasm for Liszt, which was kindled early, was fresh and

* Written in Berlin, November 1910, for the programme of the third of the Nikisch Concerts.

imitative, I transcribed the Spanish Rhapsody symphonically after Liszt's model of Schubert's Piano Fantasy (*The Wanderer*) and Weber's Polonaise arranged for piano and orchestra. It was at that time of my life when I had become conscious of such deficiencies and faults in my own playing that with energetic determination I began the study of the pianoforte again from the beginning on quite a new basis. Liszt's works were my guide and through them I acquired an intimate knowledge of his particular method. Out of his "tenets" I constructed my "technique". Gratitude and admiration made Liszt at that time my master and my friend. The Spanish Rhapsody in its original form, for pianoforte alone, puts the greatest demand on the player without affording him the possibility—even with the best success—of moving to the climaxes in a sufficiently brilliant light. These obstacles lie in the composition, the shortcomings of the instrument and the limited endurance of the pianist. Moreover, the national character of the piece requires shades of colour such as only the orchestra can give. The remodelling of this piece gives greater opportunity to the pianist for bringing out his individual style. The virtuosi who lived before the penultimate generation really played nothing but their own compositions and other works with their own alterations; they played what they had put in order for themselves, what came "pat" to them and only what they themselves could do as regards feeling as well as technique. And the public went to Paganini in order to hear Paganini (and not something by Beethoven). Today virtuosi must be quick-change artists: the spiritual tension which the *salto-mortale* from a Beethoven Hammerklavier Sonata to a Liszt Rhapsody demands is quite another achievement than that of pure pianoforte playing in itself. Thus in the virtuoso sense transcriptions are suiting another's ideas to the personality of the transcriber. With weak personalities such transcriptions become weak pictures of stronger originals, and mediocrity, which is always in the majority, brought forth, during the virtuosi period, a great number of mediocre and even tasteless and distorted transcriptions. Music like this gave transcription a bad name and forced it into an altogether subordinate position. It is only necessary to mention J. S. Bach in order, with one decisive blow, to raise the rank of the transcription to artistic honour in the reader's estimation. He was one of the most prolific arrangers of his own and other pieces, especially as organist. From him I learnt to recognise the truth that Good and Great Universal Music remains the same through whatever medium it is sounded. But also the second truth, that different mediums each have a different language (their own) in which this music again sounds somewhat differently.

Vivaldi's concertos, Schubert's songs, Weber's *Invitation to the Waltz* are still there in each case, when changed over to Bach's organ, Liszt's pianoforte, Berlioz' orchestra. But where does the transcription begin? A second Liszt setting of his Spanish Rhapsody exists which bears the title *Great Fantasy on Spanish Airs*. It is another piece; there are, in part, the same themes. Which of them is the transcription? The one which was written later? But is not the first one already an arrangement of a Spanish folk-song? That Spanish Fantasy commences with a theme which tallies with the dance motive in Mozart's *Figaro* and Mozart took this from someone else too. It is not his, it is transcribed. Moreover the same theme appears again in Gluck's ballet *Don Juan*.

The frequent opposition aroused by my transcriptions and the opposition which senseless criticism often evoked in me made me try to reach some clarity on this point.

My final opinion about it is this: that notation is itself the transcription of an abstract idea.

The moment that the pen takes possession of it the thought loses its original form. The intention of writing down an idea necessitates already a choice of time and key. The composer is obliged to decide on the form and the key and they determine more and more clearly the course to be taken and the limitations. Even if much of the idea is original and indestructible and continues to exist this will be pressed down from the moment of decision, into the type belonging to a class. The idea becomes a sonata or a concerto; this is already an arrangement of the original. From this first transcription to the second is a comparatively short and unimportant step. Yet, in general, people make a fuss only about the second. In doing so they overlook the fact that a transcription does not destroy the original; so there can be no question of loss arising from it. The performance of a work is also a transcription, and this too—however free the performance may be—can never do away with the original. For the musical work of art exists whole and intact before it has sounded and after the sound is finished.

It is, at the same time, in and outside of Time.

Most of Beethoven's pianoforte compositions, moreover, sound like transcriptions from the orchestra and most of Schumann's orchestral works sound like arrangements from the pianoforte—and they *are* so in certain ways.

For some curious reason variation form is held in great esteem by serious musicians.

This is odd, because if the variation form is built up on a borrowed theme, it produces a whole series of transcriptions and the more regardless of the theme they are, the more ingenious is the type of variation. Thus, *arrangements* are not permitted because they change the original whereas the *variation* is permitted although it *does change* the original. This Spanish Rhapsody consists of two named parts (*Folies d'Espagne—Jota Aragonese*) which are followed by an unknown third part and finale.

First of all there is the "preludising" Cadenza and variations on a slow dance theme which is alleged to be by Corelli (here again we are put in doubt over the question of transcription). This first part is in C sharp minor. The second part in D major also has variations, this time on a lively eight-bar little dance tune in 3/8 time (Glinka has also used it for an orchestral piece).

A new cadenza which touches on the coming motive leads

to the third part which has the following motive in the content:

Ex. 4

(We meet this in Mahler's third Symphony—how does it come there?)

The three themes mingle then with intensification and brilliance to an ever-increasing stretto.

We have been able to bring the motive material of both Spanish Fantasies by Liszt in conjunction with the names of Mozart, Gluck, Corelli, Glinka, Mahler. My humble name too, is now added. The human being can certainly not create, he can only employ what is in existence on the earth. And for the musician there are sounds and rhythms in existence.

With the transcription for piano and orchestra there are three kinds of settings—piano alone, orchestra alone, piano with orchestra. In the third case again there are three kinds of remodelling possible:

1. To divide the original between orchestra and piano.
2. To leave the original to the piano and give what is new to the orchestra.
3. To give the original to the orchestra and give what is new to the piano.

The choice and decision for the actual form of remodelling to employ can be determined solely through the feeling and taste of the transcriber.

There are no rules but there are models and—generally—much too much routine.

MOZART'S *DON GIOVANNI* AND LISZT'S *DON JUAN* FANTASY*

IN the valuable and charming work *Das Kloster* by Scheible (Stuttgart, 1846) the "Eilfte Zeller" gives an account of Don

* Written in Zürich, June 1917, as a preface to the *Grosse Kritische Instruktions-Ausgabe* of Liszt's *Don Juan* fantasy (Breitkopf & Härtel, 1918).

Juan Tenorio of Seville in legend and poetry. The writer, a diligent compiler, cannot refrain from introducing this paragraph:

> I presume that my readers know Mozart's masterpiece *Don Giovanni*. . . . A legend (he continues later) which after that of Faust, is one of the most important and which, in Germany, was given importance by Mozart, in the same way as that of Faust became important through Goethe.
>
> This Don Juan, a dissolute person and libertine of the first rank, came from the old Seville family, Tenorio; he is said also to have murdered the Governor of Seville who crossed his path in an amorous adventure. The bust or stone statue of the Governor was put up in a chapel of the San Francisco monastery in Seville and Juan Tenorio, at the instigation of the Governor's revengeful family, was decoyed there and murdered by the monks of the monastery. The monks then spread about the report that Don Juan had blasphemed in front of the statue in the chapel and because of that he had been fetched away by the devil.
>
> The Spanish dramatic poet, Tirso de Molina, used this material for the first time, for his play entitled *El Burlador de Sevilla y Convidado de Piedra*.

Meyer's *Konversationslexikon* (4th Edition, 1890) dedicates a special and detailed article to Don Juan. As opposed to Scheible's statement we learn from this article that earlier the Don Juan legend:

> . . . had been adapted and, under the title *El ateista fulminado*, had been performed throughout the monasteries for a long time. The first writer of any note to represent it in drama was the monk Gabriel Tellez, who lived under the name of Tirso de Molina, and was the beloved comic poet during the first half of the seventeenth century and

who used this fertile material for the stage under the title
El burlador de Sevilla y convidado de piedra.

Between these and up to Molière's *Le festin de pierre* five
arrangements of the original drama have become well known.
Corneille produced it in verse (1677), an Englishman Shadwell
and the Italian Goldoni made use of the material, and then
music took possession of it (ballet by Gluck, opera by Righini).
Finally Mozart, in 1787, in association with the poet Da Ponte,
bestowed upon the world *Il dissoluto punito ossia il Don Giovanni.*

That this opera should be almost the only one to keep its
position on the stage for 130 years is such an extraordinary
event in the history of the theatre that it relieves the editor
from the enumeration of its excellencies. Nevertheless, he has
observed that Mozart's work, spoken of with reverence,
listened to with devotion and delight, encounters an unexpected indifference amongst many present-day musicians,
which he can only explain thus; that a standard of knowledge
and culture such as is not often to be met with in musicians is
essential for the complete appreciation of Mozart's scores. To
the "Wagner" generation particularly the text and music of
Don Giovanni seem to be "simple" and colourless. For the
educated world the pure lines of the Antique had been adul-
terated by the Baroque.

It is thanks to the younger German conductors that Mozart
held his ground through and beyond this crisis: attracted by
the great value of the scores they studied them enough to
wonder at them and were compelled to love them too—what
public will ever have that capacity? They produced the masterpieces again and again and the more trouble they took the
deeper was their satisfaction.

I have, personally, an objection to raise against the excellently made libretto of the Abbé Lorenzo da Ponte, which is
that the hero is not represented as being victorious enough,
that his amorous successes in the piece are not even brilliant,
and in addition to this, he turns out to be more malleable than

demoniacal. In the tedious character of Donna Elvira, who crosses his path, he is encumbered with the consequence of an old "liaison". (Don Giovanni's personality should be so towering and intimidating, where it does not appear in the capacity of wooer, that a woman who wished to accuse him would never venture near him.) If Donna Anna does not lie, then Don Giovanni courted her in vain. The most serious and threatening situation arises from his little flirtation with the peasant girl. Finally, it is for the murder, and not for his lasciviousness that Don Giovanni goes to his destruction, according to Da Ponte.

By paraphrasing the three most important moments in the opera, Liszt, guided by his excellent instincts, has attempted to underline the "demoniacal" (which lies nearer the 1830 epoch than Mozart's time). The choice of these three moments from the whole opera is significant of his unerring perception of what is important in it. In this kind of thing Liszt never failed; he knew how to choose the "catch phrase" for the impression he aimed at, and how to appeal to the public. He knew the force of a striking quotation and it is not by chance that he begins his *Dante* Symphony with the verse "Per me si và nella città dolente". Springing from the ground of salon music and of opera pot-pourris, both of which forms the stupendous pianistic achievements of the young Liszt had outgrown, we willingly agree with the strict purists who maintain that the *Don Juan* Fantasy treats sacred themes in altogether too worldly a fashion. On the other hand, this piece among pianists has acquired the almost symbolic significance of a pianistic summit and this makes it obligatory to study it aesthetically. The remarks at the foot of the printed music will carry out these aims in our task. We give these few preliminary ones in advance however.

Liszt's well-bred opera fantasy is distinguishable from the plebeian pot-pourri by its well-considered choice of themes, by its systematic arrangement of form and contrasts, and by the effort to expand and fill out the motives which are chosen.

Liszt's opera fantasies in general are built up in three parts.

The piece opens with a detailed introduction, solemn or atmosphere-producing, followed by a lyrical middle episode, from which a bridge is thrown, generally by a modulating, hastening episode (in which the earlier and the coming motives appear) to the Finale which constitutes a movement of more lively character.[1]

The ornamental decoration, to which Liszt's majestic mastery of all the possibilities of the pianoforte lends a luxuriant development, is used only in the most rare cases as an end in itself. It is usually employed for characterisation.

Where this assertion does not appear to be true—possibly to the average player and to the non-playing students of aesthetics —they should reflect, when reading or playing it, that what appears to them as a too luxuriant growth was to Liszt an easy task which he overcame and presented unobtrusively.

Therefore, I recommend every pianist, most urgently, while playing it (and from the first moment of studying it) to keep the transparency and economy of Mozart's *Don Juan* continually before his eyes, and to strive for this as the final aim of the interpretation. (In certain places where, otherwise, it might be almost impossible to find a solution of the problem some simplifications of the piano setting have been made in the editor's arrangement.)

This piece of advice is all the more worthy of consideration because pianists not only wish to make an ostentatious piece out of the fantasy but for the most part cannot do otherwise. But merely to master the difficulties does not count, they must be surmounted with grace; and they must not be put on show at all.

[1] As a more concrete example: if it were a question of the paraphrase of *Carmen*, the transcriber, following Liszt's example, would begin with the suggestive scene in the market place in Act IV, and in the introduction as contrast to this, would join the pathetic "Carmen" theme built on the gipsy scale. The middle section would be composed of the Habanera (followed by variations), the Finale, the bull-ring music. When Liszt could not exhaust all the motives or dramatic content in a single paraphrase he did not hesitate to lavish two or more Fantasies on the same work; for example *Lucrezia Borgia* (2), *Lucia* (3), Meyerbeer's *Propheten* (4).

Although there are earlier and later versions of all Liszt's earlier pianoforte works, Liszt never made a revision of this fantasy, so we must suppose that he regarded this first edition as definitive.[1]

On the other hand Liszt wrote an edition of the same work for two pianos, which to the editor seems to throw a flood of light on Liszt's later manner of thinking. Transparency, unforcedness, and the neglect of what is pathetic, here come nearer to the original Mozart in the sense that the editor has in mind as worth striving for. Some of the variations, also, are musically interesting enough for them to be quoted in the footnotes.

During the lifelong course of his pianistic studies the editor has always endeavoured to simplify the mechanism of piano playing and to reduce it to what is absolutely indispensable in movement and expenditure of strength. His mature opinion is that the acquirement of a technique is nothing else than fitting a given difficulty to one's own capacities. That this will be furthered to a lesser extent through physical practising and to a greater extent through keeping an eye on the task mentally is a truth which perhaps has not been obvious to every pianoforte pedagogue, but surely it is obvious to every player who attains his aim through self-education and reflection.

It is not through attacking the difficulty repeatedly but through the examination of the problem that success in solving it is possible.[2]

The principle remains a general one, but the execution of it demands at times a new adaptation, an individual nuance.

[1] The fact that "Nouvelle édition revue par l'Auteur" is printed on the title page of the second edition must not confuse us. Comparison with the original edition shows us the illusion. For out of the four opera fantasies which (having first been published singly) were published together as one work in the second edition, only one Die Hugenotten went through an intensive rearrangement. Die Jüdin and Robert der Teufel (besides Don Juan) belong to this group. The Don Juan Fantasy originally published by Schlesinger, had the dedication "A Sa Majesté Chrétien VIII Frédérice Roi de Danemark respectueux et reconnaissant hommage F. Liszt."

[2] Assuming, of course, a reasonably well-disciplined gift.

Thus the editor has placed the version of the fantasy which
suits him, under Liszt's unchanged original text, not as a conclusive model, but merely as the result of his own experiences
which are for him decisive. By doing this he wished to give an
instance of how one can and should arrange a setting for oneself without distorting the sense, content and effect.

THE TRANSCRIPTION*

TRANSCRIPTION occupies an important place in the literature of the piano; and looked at from a right point of view,
every important piano piece is the reduction of a big thought
to a practical instrument. But transcription has become an
independent art; no matter whether the starting-point of a
composition is original or unoriginal. Bach, Beethoven, Liszt,
and Brahms were evidently all of the opinion that there is
artistic value concealed in a pure transcription, for they all
cultivated the art themselves, seriously and lovingly. In fact,
the art of transcription has made it possible for the piano to
take possession of the entire literature of music. Much that is
inartistic, however, has got mixed up with this branch of the
art. And it was because of the cheap, superficial estimation of
it made by certain men, who had to hide their nakedness with
a mantle of "being serious", that it sank down to what was
considered a low level.

* Letter to his wife, 22nd July 1913.

V

BACH

BACH'S art today still continues to be the middle point between the prehistoric and the present in musical creations. Like his successors, Mozart and Beethoven, Bach committed some of his most valuable thoughts to the keyboard, that discredited, indispensable and most comprehensive of all instruments.

Modern times have taken possession of the instrument as well as the master with increasing interest and understanding; both become more alive the further and more deeply one penetrates into them. The rejuvenated pianoforte gives birth again to the master of the pianoforte, and behind what are only apparently old-fashioned forms it reveals the soul of a great man.

Everything is multiform and vigorous here, and what is technical is placed without effort at the service of the chosen thoughts, foreshadowing much that is still in the future today, and setting a seal on its own epoch.

THE FUGUE

On Board the "Rotterdam", January 1915

BACH allowed twenty years to elapse between the publication of the first and second part of the *Well-tempered Clavier*, and it is about twenty years since I began to make notes of my reflections about the work. An intelligent reader, therefore, will expect to find that the treatment of the second part will show a different physiognomy from that of the earlier one; he

* Shortened introduction to the Bach edition for Breitkopf & Härtel. Written in Zürich, 20th October 1915.

must himself comprehend this volume with different assumptions and with maturer preparation.

Here I purposely avoid repetitions of earlier arguments and turn aside from what is purely pianistic, as from a theme which, in the five previous volumes of my Bach studies, has come under discussion in detail; I have not lingered over (or shortened) details of less importance; to have done so would distract the attention from the principal moments and above all I have endeavoured to conduct the learner to the mysteries of the musical structure and to lead him within.

Although, with great display of dignity, the fugue is called the strictest form in musical composition, it must in my opinion be allowed the widest freedom if it is to continue in undiminished vigour. I have never come across an absolutely strict fugue amongst works which lay claim to artistic (not merely formal) value. To me it seems much more as if an increase of freedom keeps step with the ascent to artistic preeminence.

There is, perhaps, no fugue which does not cease to be one at moments. A really strict fugue would be a polyphonic structure that never deviated from the theme and in which no voice ever paused. This would be the ideal type of strict fugue —to which as yet no artist has kept unconditionally—resembling a bird that circles uninterruptedly in the air.

Even the Bach fugue (for him, the most homogeneous form for expressing feeling) is rich in irregularities and "exceptions". The theorists are compelled, with embarrassment, to mention these instances. And if I must agree with them that only the superiority of a master gives such rights of freedom, it follows, quite as decidedly, that it is at the acquisition of these very rights that mastery aims.

The accepted rules for writing a fugue are partly practical and partly of symbolic origin. Thus, practically, the formation of the "answer" is carried out in relation to a prescribed circle of modulation.

The symbolism of the laws can be summed up in the axiom: harmony in combat, equal rights accorded to all voices united in the fundamental idea.

The final aim of the fugue, both practical and symbolic, is the exploitation of the fundamental idea up to the point of its exhaustion.

In the present-day art of composition, which is descended in a straight line from that of Bach (in so far as it strives more and more consciously through polyphony to become feeling in sound) the course of moving towards the middle point of the modulation circle—dependence on key—and objective symbolism both fall out of the plan which makes way for the subjective temperament. Consequently the Master's rights have been extended; he may now take possession of the Bach exceptions as rules.

The form of the fugue, above all, will always be dependent on the nature of the theme. Bach points out this truth to us often enough, but at times he is found in opposition to it. But the impetus of the theme lies in its own productiveness and its susceptibility to alteration.

The second impetus is the spiritual idea which moves the fugue inwardly, and a third, the range of feeling which envelops it as it moves forward.

The fugue, to Beethoven, was no longer the natural expression of his feeling in general, but a tool to be employed when feeling took a particular direction. It is conceivable that in the fugue of today the counter-subject may triumph over the theme; or that the form may imperceptibly pass over into other forms, dissolving instead of consolidating, or that the theme, out of a multiform movement, may come forth as a final issue.

Among the fugues in this volume those in D major and E flat major stand nearest to the true type.

In my remarks I have passed over the first for artistic reasons and unreservedly appreciated the second; because here the spirit is manifest through the scholastic medium. Yet, because it derives new forms from the fundamental idea, the regular fugue in F sharp minor awakens a purer pleasure in me although it leaves out of consideration many thematic combinations (which I have set down in examples). The B flat minor fugue, uniting the happiest idea with the most perfect construction, is an unqualified masterpiece. The fugues in D minor, in E minor, and in A minor, represent the power of temperament over reflection; the "Dance" fugue in B flat major remains a single bloom of grace and softened austerity.

The fugues in F minor and F major give delight as polyphonic dance forms. Likewise the three-part fugue in B minor, which captures the spirit of a spring dance. The double fugue in G sharp minor takes a solitary position; with great beauty of form, and closest unity of modulations, the effect it produces is one full of the finest feeling.

The relationship of the obligatory prelude to its fugue does not seem to me to be established clearly enough. The preludes of the *Well-tempered Clavier* obviously do not make it easy for one to become more certain over this question. As editor I have devoted some diligence to establishing a definite connection between prelude and fugue, occasionally showing this by means of examples. In the later examples I believe I have overstepped Bach's intentions.

All changes and additions, however, follow the educational intention of giving the learner an insight into the mechanism of the composition. Moreover they illustrate and supplement the views only sketchily set out in the introduction. It is only the sum of the remarks on different pieces which, in many cases, at last form a complete opinion about one and the same question.

BACH'S TOCCATAS*

IT seems almost as if a greater freedom and toleration used to

* Introduction to Bach's Toccatas, in Vol. XVIII of the Bach-Busoni edition. Written in Zürich, August 1916.

prevail amongst the older musicians than is the case today; thus, it was allowable to give the title "Toccata" to pieces of varying content and with forms diverging widely one from another. The three Toccatas with which we are here concerned, prove this again. Many Toccatas have one thing in common—that they are compiled from a number of different smaller forms, and another is that they aim at velocity and bravura. But what do we arrive at if we wish to form an invariable rule from this observation? With such a limitation how do we rank the organ Toccata in C major which is majestic, rich in feeling, and bold? And how does it rank with that exercise and piece for endurance by Schumann, op. 7? Praised be freedom which is the true sanctuary of art. Therefore in the Toccata, the "Concert Piece", everyone is allowed to find or give that which is in his own heart. The Toccata stands nearest to improvisation. Improvisation would stand nearest the true essence of art if it lay within human capacity to master its promptings. The Toccata certainly consists in improvisation and reflection, momentary ideas and elaboration, easily inclining towards fluency, feeling, or form; tarrying here, quickly breaking off there, playing transiently from one to the other and mostly without the pretension of representing anything permanent.

Stated briefly, of the three Toccatas submitted, the one in E minor consists of two preludes and fugues in succession. The middle one in G minor is formed differently. Introduced and finished off by a run, it divides into two movements, the first a three-part movement (Adagio, Allegro, Adagio) followed by a somewhat talkative and successful fugue.

The third Toccata (G major) stands in complete opposition to both its forerunners, with its unmistakable character of a concerto (Italian) and its three typical movements.

Apart from the inevitable fact that the fugue is never missing we recognise a decided independence in the forms of the Bach pianoforte and organ Toccatas which rejoices the artist just as much as it confuses the theorist.

BACH

SKETCH FOR A DRAMATIC PERFORMANCE
OF BACH'S ST. MATTHEW PASSION*

IT was Herr von Herzogenberg who sent me to the St.
Matthew Passion for the first time for the furtherance of my
musical education. Even at that time I was struck by the
dramatic force of the recitatives (very much to the dissatisfaction of Herr von Herzogenberg who meant it for my good
and who wished me to give most of my attention to the chorals).
For years these recitatives and the moving choruses fostered
in me the wish to draw up and, if possible, to see a dramatic
performance of the Bach Passion. The difficulties which stand
in the way of this plan are considerable. Unlike the so-called
"Heights of Calvary" which lead the pilgrim through twelve
stations in a spiral ascent to the summit, where the three crosses,
visible from afar, terminate the tragedy of suffering, Bach's
musical illustration is to be compared rather to a frieze on
which the events are portrayed one after another, in a straight
line.

This arrangement gives the possibility of abridgments in the
same measure as it admits the possibility of endless extension.
Systematic groups returning as on strips of tapestry divide
them into narrative, action, contemplation, and moral; these
four groups follow each new event, like stations on a level
tract. The moral is announced through the chorus in the four-
part chorale, and the contemplation is inserted in the form of an
aria. Apart from the fact that the arias delay the action unduly,
and interrupt it, the odd sanctimonious setting of the words of
the text in these arias is opposed aesthetically to that of the
Evangelist's chronicle.

However successful many of them are in form and feeling
(especially in their position) anyone making a dramatic arrangement would be obliged to apply the scissors here and
remove the arias without a moment's hesitation. To sacrifice

* Written in Berlin, December 1921, for the magazine *Faust*, Vol. III.

the detail to the whole is one of the most imperative duties of form in art (although one of the most painful).

When once the arias are rejected, there remain the narrative, the action, and the chorus singing. With the swift conciseness of the Evangelist's account the events seen should move so quickly that they tumble over one another. To lend rhythm and clearness to the intricate tempo, the two stages placed one over the other, which are to be seen in the primitive sketch,

should be of service. Through it we acquire space and simultaneousness. Between these stages, half a storey high, the chorus sits right and left; in the middle pulpit stands the narrator, dominating all, and at the same time acting as the centre from which the threads of the action and score extend, radiating in all directions. The fixed position of the chorus affords the convenience of the beginning or after effect of a dramatic chapter being enacted in dumb show while they sing.

Care should be taken on the one hand to be sure that the

space displayed brings a concentrated, intimate (and at the same time uniform and unchangeable) character to the whole with the harmony of a gothic cathedral, but the piece cut out (through which the upper stage appears) gives the horizon as a background, and suggests a public street and the possibility of thinking of an incident as being played "out-of-doors".

VI

MOZART

MOZART: APHORISMS*

I WRITE down the following notes at this time when every musician turns his thoughts to Mozart. Subjective and hardly exhaustive though they may be, they help to portray the characteristics of the more or less definite picture which all cultured people have in themselves of the personality of the "divine Master". I send the notes to you in the simple form in which they arose.

I think of Mozart thus:

Up to now he is the most complete manifestation of musical gifts. Every genuine musician looks up to him, happy and disarmed.

His short life and his fertility lift his perfection to the rank of the phenomenal.

His never-clouded beauty disconcerts.

His sense of form is also supernatural.

His art is like a sculptor's masterpiece—presenting from every side a finished picture.

He has the instinct of an animal, setting himself tasks to tax his strength to the utmost limits, but no further.

He dares nothing foolhardy.

He finds without seeking and does not seek what is unfindable—perhaps what would be unfindable to him.

His resources are extraordinarily abundant, but he never uses them all.

He can say very much, but he never says too much.

*Written for the 150th anniversary of Mozart's birth, for the *Lokal Anzeiger*, Berlin, 1906.

He is passionate, but keeps to the forms of chivalry.

He bears all characters in himself, but only as presenter and portrayer.

He gives the solution with the riddle.

His proportions are astoundingly correct, but they can be measured and verified.

He disposes of light and shadow, but his light does not pain and his darkness still shows clear outlines.

Even in the most tragic situations he still has a witticism ready, in the most cheerful he is able to draw a thoughtful furrow in his brow.

He is universal through his dexterity.

He can continue to draw from every glass because he has never drunk to the bottom of one.

He stands so high that he sees further than all and sees everything, therefore, somewhat diminished.

His palace is immeasurably big, but he never steps outside its walls.

Through its windows he sees nature; the window frame is also her frame.

Joy is his most outstanding feature; his smile decks with flowers even what is most unpleasant.

His smile is not that of a diplomat or actor, but of a pure spirit—and yet man of the world.

His spirit is not pure out of ignorance.

He has not remained simple and not become cunning.

He is full of temperament without any nervousness.

Idealist without losing touch with the earth, realist without ugliness.

He is a burgher as well as an aristocrat, but never boor or demagogue.

He is a friend of Order: miracle and sorcery preserve their sixteen and thirty-two bars.

He is religious in so far as religion is identical with harmony.

In him the antique and rococo combine in perfect ways without resulting in a new architecture.

Architecture is next of kin to his art.

He is not demoniacal and not supernatural, his realism is of this earth.

He is the complete and round number, the perfect sum, a conclusion and no beginning.

He is young as a boy and wise as an old man—never old-fashioned and never modern, carried to the grave and always alive.

His smile, which was so human, still shines on us trans-figured.

FOR THE *DON GIOVANNI* JUBILEE*

WHILST many maintain that the boundary between talent and genius is so difficult to draw because one is unable to recognise the transition from one to the other, others contend that talent and genius are two completely different things, things that not only have nothing in common but are so opposed that great care must be taken not to exchange or con-fuse one with the other. The conceptions of the matter are so endlessly different and yet all of such a nature that of two plausible theories one destroys the other, and in each a dark unvanquishable point hinders further investigation. This point is the manner of the activity of our brain in general and during the process of creation in particular. Unfortunately, one must assume that the solution of this problem (which would bring with it the final explanation of the conception of "mind" and what hangs together with it) will not be found and—it seems to me—for two reasons. First, we have no possible means of observing an existing human brain in activity; observation of animals who have no activity of thought would be of no avail. Secondly, it is not possible to make this observation mentally, that is, by means of one's own thought, for in order to do this it is necessary to make use of just that brain activity which we

* Written for the *Neue Zeitschrift für Musik*, Leipzig, 26th October 1887.

wish to investigate, and in this case one movement must counteract the other and neutralise the activity itself. This attempt, in my opinion, is as little possible as it is possible for a man to see his own eye without the help of a glass, or a sleeper to follow the process of sleep while he puts it into effect himself. Some contemporary thinkers on the subject take their stand on fanciful hypotheses, but they show how impossible the investigation is even more clearly than those who attempt to find a scientific basis for research. The consideration of the nature of talent and genius has offered a better prospect of success.

Schopenhauer took talent to be an "excess of intuition", but genius has such an abounding excess of intuition that it becomes to a very great extent identical with the will.

The difference, according to this, is one of quantity. Max Nordau opposes this view in his able manner in the following sentences: "Talent is shown in performing what most or many people do without being able to acquire the same dexterity. . . . Genius is shown in discovering new activities never practised before or practising old ones in a quite unique and personal method. . . . A poodle whom one can train to perform more complicated tricks than other dogs has talent. . . . Between talent and genius arises not a difference of quantity but of quality."

Yet in the end Nordau is also obliged to admit that "the distinction between the different degrees of greatness rests on the same characteristics" and that "Mont Blanc and a grain of quartz sand merely differ from one another in quantity but at the bottom are one and the same thing".

According to Lemcke it is the mode and method with which the artist proceeds in his creation which shows whether he has talent or genius. Lemcke's theory includes the simple conceptions of naïveté and reflection, and according to this principle the achievement of what is new and original in art would still only be the work of talent in so far as that can be achieved through reflection. His theory is that perfection is the mark of genius as long as it is obtained intuitively and even though by means already in existence. But Nordau, who looks for the new to arise only in genius, distinguishes further between emotional and cogitative genius—he gives precedence to the latter in which he places in descending order, Commanders-in-Chief, statesmen, legislators, researchers, discoverers and inventors, thinkers and philosophers; in the second category, emotional genius, in the order of precedence, poets, artists and musicians—through which, of course, the doctrine of naïveté and contemplation as characteristics of talent and genius becomes weakened once more.

My opinion is that a work of art in which content and form are united in equal perfection is always a product of genius whether it arose unconsciously or through reflection and in so far as it does not obviously betray deliberation and elaboration. Such are the works of Raphael, Dürer, Lessing, Goethe, Beethoven, Mozart.

The question, however, remains for the most part as little solved as, for instance, that which concerns the difference between the sublime and the beautiful, and since these terms will often be mentioned in the course of my essay I will attempt a short discussion on the difference between them.

Is the sublime merely the enhancement of beauty through the enlargement of the scale of proportions or is it an independent idea? When Lemcke in his popular aesthetic says that "the sublime is that which is governed by the measure which defies measurement", he answers the first question in the affirmative, since by "measure" he means only what is connected with beauty. Must the sublime always be beautiful and cannot ugliness often produce the sublime?

A thunderstorm unchained in all its power, the fall of an avalanche, indeed the conflagration of an extensive village can produce a sublime impression. Although they are neither beautiful[1]—according to the aesthete's ideas—nor are they governed by measurement. The view of a quiet lake or the

[1] When the word beautiful is used it will always mean aesthetic beauty.

sunset in a mountain landscape perhaps meet these conditions better; whilst moments out of the last movement of Beethoven's Ninth Symphony, for instance, are sublime in the sense of the thunderstorm and the avalanche.

But on the other hand, do the measurements of the sublime always exceed our measure? Is it not more often the kind rather than the magnitude of a thought that makes it sublime? The Commendatore's admonishing words in the cemetery scene of Mozart's masterpiece, with their measured rhythms and full chords on the trombones between the free sentences of the secco recitatives, effect the sublime through the strength of the position which they occupy and the contrast following therefrom.

If we compare Beethoven's nature with the grandeur of a thunderstorm, Mozart's is like an eternal sunny day. Whether this day irradiates a laughing meadow or the mighty sea, or a rocky desert, it is continually brilliant, joyful, clear. If cheerful serenity and simplicity are characteristics of genius Mozart possessed them in full measure. In fact no one could lay claim to genius with greater justice than Mozart. His works speak, sound and exist as conclusive evidence of this. All theories are useless, aesthetics in vain, philosophising idle, when confronted with the power of this language, the fact of this enduring reality. Yes, as far as music is concerned our musical theories, aesthetics and philosophies depend to a great extent on three things only: they are the continuation and the fulfilled necessity of these magnificent musical creations.

To the naïve question repeatedly asked by the dilettante, "Who is the greatest of all musicians?" I have never given an answer because the question—which apparently demands only the mere pronunciation of a name—would in fact have to be extended to the length of a popular lecture on aesthetics. But if an answer must be given, the name is Mozart.

At the risk of being obliged to bring forward things already well known and accepted as final, and which through time and experience have been long confirmed, I cannot refrain—to express myself philosophically—from attempting the *a priori* proof of this empirical fact.

The greatness of Mozart, unrivalled up to now, shows itself above all in its many-sidedness. In every sphere and in every branch of music he produced perfection, he achieved absolute beauty, he knew how to set up a model of style, he succeeded in forming something complete and finished of which his models only contained a suggestion.

He was a lyrical, a dramatic, liturgical and absolute musician. He was an absolute musician always and without exception, and one of the most distinctive marks of his creative art is that his manner of composition adapts his phrase to the text with admirable faithfulness while keeping its complete value as a piece of music.

With his sonatas he expanded pianoforte technique. With the concertos he prepared the way, above all, for the present-day importance and independence of the instrument. With his string quartets he brought depth and content into Haydn's ingenuous four-part writing for strings without any sacrifice of cheerfulness; he brought the orchestra to its complete expression in his symphonies and gave them that monumental form which Beethoven worked on and chiselled to gigantic proportions in his last four colossal odd-number symphonies.

With the Ave Verum and the Requiem, Mozart gave the purest and truest musical embodiment of the Catholic ideas of blessedness and death, resurrection and punishment. Finally he handled with the same unrivalled success comedy, drama, and as its originator, German Grand Opera.

Obviously, Mozart takes song as his starting point through which the uninterrupted melodic form shows itself and this shimmers through his phrases like beautiful feminine forms through the folds of light drapery. One follows, for example, in his scores, the second voice of a woodwind ensemble—it is continuously the alto of a four-part song, subordinate certainly through position and order but not in the melodic arrangement. And it is this stream of song which forms Mozart's contrapuntal phrases so easily and pleasingly that, far from hearing the labour of composition even in the strictest development, one is sensible of the purest happiness and satisfaction. If you listen to one of those very characteristic progressions which are a wonderful network of harmonic delicacy, contrapuntal facility, and melodic structure you will find yourself transposed into a mood which holds you mid-way between crying and laughing, owing to the way in which it moves and exhilarates you at the same time.[1]

With Mozart, ease of execution goes hand-in-hand with ease of conception and comprehension, and it is truly astounding how even with the simplest means he always chooses and divines what is right.

It is, for instance, an easy thing for him in an unbroken sixteen-bar period to bring in the individualism of two or even several characters where any other composer, with great effort perhaps, would have piled up two or three different themes next to or on top of each other and in this way disfigured the construction of the period. I remember, just for example, the malicious remarks interpolated by Don Giovanni and Leporello in Donna Elvira's first aria ("Do you understand? A Beauty deserted by the beloved", and so on), the appeal "Beautiful young lady" introduced in a masterly way as coda, the quartet "Non ti fidar o misera" and, above all, the last scene where Mozart repeatedly builds up the musical characteristics of Don Giovanni's knightly defiance and Leporello's comical fear and the Commendatore's spiritual austerity in one sentence without interrupting the period.

Through the mastery and unusually beautiful treatment of form Mozart's settings attain that peculiar aesthetic calm which (if in discussing western music the thought of a relationship with Hellenic art is at all allowable) might lead one to draw a parallel between this and Mozart's settings.

[1] I need not remind the reader of the glorious examples in *The Magic Flute* (Overture, Song of the Men in Armour) or the Finale of the "Jupiter" Symphony.

The following quotation strengthens the comparison: "Holding important means of expression in reserve for an important dramatic moment."—Rietz writes thus in his preface to the *Don Giovanni* edition edited by him. This is a procedure which Mozart knows how to employ in the most effective way: through the symmetrical relationships of his form, within the separate pieces, as also in their relationship to one another through the architecturally organised building up of the orchestral period, and finally through that restraint in the measure of beauty, even in the highest moments of tragedy and of the most violent passion, which falsely is often used as a reproach against Mozart—only by people of limited intelligence, it is true—as being a deficiency in the power of expression, and which Lessing defines with such enlightening logic as one of the most important merits of the Laokoon group.

As an illustration to show that I have allied myself to more important and authoritative men in my attempted comparison, I will quote from the preface by Rietz already mentioned: "On the 29th December 1797 Schiller wrote to Goethe: 'I always had a certain confidence in opera and believed that tragedy would develop out of it as it did out of the old choruses of the Bacchus feasts.' Whereupon Goethe answered on the following day: 'The hope which you had of the opera you would have seen realised at last in a high degree in *Don Giovanni* but this work is unique and Mozart's death has put an end to the expectation of anything equal to it.'"

Born a German, educated as an Italian, and in his early days thrown under the influence of a Master—Gluck—with a strong leaning towards the French, Mozart absorbed the teaching and rules of all three schools, without especially leaning to one more than another in his creative art.

Subsequently his musical character developed free from all mannerisms, and destitute of every national gloss, to that independence and objectivity which has its inevitable result in the production of an absolute work of art. This work in spite of differences of language, customs and times has, for a hundred years, maintained its position among all cultured nations with such freshness and vigour that it is still an unfailing and invaluable stimulus to performers, translators and scholars. And so far no limit can be put to its length of life. To this work—*Don Giovanni*—we will dedicate the second half of our critical study.

"Il dissoluto punito ossia Il Don Giovanni
Dramma giocoso in due atti
La Poesia è dell'Abbate Da Ponte Poeta de'Teatri imperiali
La Musica è del Sigr Wolfgang Mozart, Maestro di Cap"

Mozart's original title runs thus, word for word.

What strikes us at once is the description "dramma giocoso"; first because of the Italian title which departs from the usual *opera buffa,* and secondly because "dramma giocoso" hardly describes the plot and the action of the opera.

Even though the comic element may be found in the tenor of the text and in the situation of the drama, yet the whole plot of the libretto speaks for the tragic character of the piece, and so especially does the fundamental thought of Sin and Punishment contained in it. Although the idea of the punishment may seem laughable at first because of Masetto's boorish undertaking having failed and because Octavio does not succeed in carrying out his threatened plans of revenge which are intended seriously for Don Giovanni anyhow, still his merited destiny overtakes the hero in the end and the greatest of his sins—the murder and mockery of the murdered man—meets the ruin which it deserves. To this moment he draws nearer and nearer with true dramatic intensity and although he persists in his ever-mounting defiance it annihilates him in the end. In Shakespeare also we meet with comic moments in tragedy, even if his fools and the boorish scenes are not so intimately involved with the action, and although his comic people throughout do not stand in such close relationship to the tragic characters of the dramas as Leporello's personality and action do to the characters of Da Ponte's drama. Yet Shakespeare has examples of this kind and it would occur to nobody—in spite of Falstaff's stronger personality—to describe his historical dramas with the epithet "jocose".

In *Don Giovanni*, out of the eight persons in the play five are serious characters (Don Giovanni, the Commendatore, Donna Anna, Don Octavio, Elvira), one charming (Zerlina), and only two (Leporello and Masetto) allotted to comedy. Out of the twenty-six musical numbers of the opera, with the most rigorous sifting, the content of only five is purely comic[1] for one can include neither the beginning of the churchyard duet, (with Leporello's droll terror which is certainly amusing and in which the Statue throws in his bass "Yes", nor the duet (Zerlina, Leporello) "Per queste tue manine", which was composed subsequently and which is regularly cut.

These five are considered, of course, apart from the numerous recitatives which often contain rather too much downright comedy without, however, affecting the musical groundplan of the opera. Nevertheless both elements, the comic and the tragic, co-exist quite distinctly in Mozart's music and even the overture shows, in its two sharply separated parts, the most dazzling contrast and—I should almost like to say—cuts the piece into the two component parts, "drama" and "comedy".

If in the separation of these two contrasting elements we find a similarity to Shakespeare, we see it even more clearly in the sharply modelled individuality of each character and in the consistent way each is followed out and kept apart.

The modest nobleness of Donna Anna stands in opposition to the mortified love of the passionate Elvira, incapable of action, and together they rise into even sharper contrast with Zerlina's naïvely sly charm.

In contrast to these three an effect is produced by the

[1] These are "Keine Ruh bei Tag und Nacht" (Leporello), "Die Registerarie", Masetto's aria "Hab's Verstanden", the duet "Gib dich Zufrieden (Leporello and Don Juan), and Don Giovanni's aria "Ihr geht Sogleich zur Rechten hin".

arrogant masculinity, the "overpowering personality"[1] of the light-hearted Don Giovanni, who could not be bent even by the terrible admonitions of his revengeful victims. Certainly Leporello (from *lepus, leporis*—really "Hare-foot") differs from Shakespeare's "clowns" in that he does not, like them, utter sharp truths and let fall worldly wisdom under the mantle of wit and play on words. But he throws, by the interpretation he puts on them, a gleam of absurdity on all the events in which he takes part.

Only once does he burst out bluntly with the truth and then only after having prudently provided for his own safety by engaging his master's word of honour.[2] The feeblest figure and the only one provoking doubt is Don Octavio; the languishing and undecided future husband of Donna Anna.

During the whole action he has really nothing else to do than to agree with her—the beloved—continually. He works through suggestion, using a physiological expression, but this only governs his intentions and cannot bring him to the point of putting them into effect. It is Donna Anna who compels him to swear revenge, who discovers her father's murderer, follows him and succeeds in unmasking him in his own house.

Most translators have honestly taken pains to rescue this

---

[1] See Max Kalbeck in his preface.

[2]

DON GIOVANNI	Well, speak. What would you tell me? Say it quickly.
LEPORELLO	Sir, What I'd say is a very serious matter.
DON GIOVANNI	It seems so.
LEPORELLO	Of serious consequence.
DON GIOVANNI	All the better. Come, out with it.
LEPORELLO	First promise that this time you will not punish me.
DON GIOVANNI	I promise, on my honour, that is, provided the Commendatore is not mentioned.
LEPORELLO	No one listens?
DON GIOVANNI	Of course not.
LEPORELLO	No one's approaching?
DON GIOVANNI	Stuff!
LEPORELLO	Then I can speak out freely, safe from your anger?
DON GIOVANNI	Yes.
LEPORELLO	Then at once I'll begin. Well, my much valued master, the life you are leading is that of a rascal!

character, and there are two places especially which offer the most delicate and yet at the same time the most favourable opportunity for vindicating Octavio's character at one blow.

I shall leave both passages in the original and follow them with the literal translation.[1] The first of them forms the end of the recitative before the aria "Il mio tesoro intanto".

1. Amici miei, dopo eccessi sì enormi dubitar non possiam che Don Giovanni non sia l'empio uccisore del padre di Donn' Anna. In questa casa per poche ore fermatevi; un ricorso vò fare a chi si deve, e in poch' istanti vendicarvi prometto; così vuole dover, pietade, affetto.—My friends, after such boundless excesses we can no longer doubt that Don Giovanni was the impious murderer of Donna Anna's father. Stop in this house a few hours. I will lodge a denunciation in due form and I promise to revenge you in a short time: this is willed by duty, piety and love.

The second passage refers to this and is at the beginning of the recitative before the so-called "Letter" aria.

2. Calmatevi, idol mio; di quel ribaldo vedrem punito in breve i gravi eccessi, vendicati sarem.—Calm yourself Beloved, soon we shall see the grievous wickedness of that abominable man punished and be revenged.

Gugler, in his edition of *Don Giovanni* published by Leckhart according to the original, changes nothing in Octavio's way of acting but justifies it in the following way.

1. Remain here in your house for your own protection for I go to accuse him of the murder. *I may not pollute my sword with the blood of this base man*, nevertheless punishment shall fall on him.

[1] I refrain from quoting the course which the action takes, leading to these two passages, taking it for granted that they are known to the reader.

2. I have arranged everything: he can no longer escape from punishment and tomorrow his destiny will over-take him.

On the other hand A. v. Wolzogen does not allow Octavio to express his purpose with regard to the legal denouncement and leaves the spectator to explain Octavio's plans according to his own comprehension.

1. Therefore follow her [Donna Anna] now and wait with her until my return. *My revenge will soon reach the guilty one. What I do so fervently desire will succeed.* Duty, love and honour require it.
2. O be comforted, Beloved. Indeed the guilty one has once more evaded my revenge but his hour is nearing.

In this point Grandaur's reading is similar, in fact, almost identical:

1. Without delay leave me to revenge you of all and to punish the guilty one.
2. Up and be comforted, O dearest one. Soon that criminal will meet with just punishment. Revenge already threatens his head.

Max Kalbeck went to work here with quite a different and much more successful method. In order to exterminate the disease under which the libretto languishes Kalbeck comes on the scene like an energetic surgeon cutting into the flesh whilst his forerunners are like country doctors prescribing homely remedies and plasters.

I refer all well-informed readers to his work but I will quote from it some passages which refer to the words of Don Octavio quoted above.

I have allowed myself to deviate from the original text

117

in the preliminary "Secco" recitative to the "Letter" aria in order to help to give the much-abused character of Don Octavio a fitting dignity. Of course only in so far as the musical side of it will not be in the least disturbed.

Don Octavio proceeding with energy to the police produces the most contemptible figure, according to the prevailing ideas of honour, and the indignant onlooker would like best to hurl a couple of rotten apples after him.

Octavio off the stage may be an incontestable knight without fear or reproach, how does that help him if he cannot bear the footlights and if in the most important scenes he shrinks into the miserable figure which we are accustomed to deplore?

No, whoever will save Don Octavio's character must set about this laudable work with the greatest decision and most ruthless energy.

At this point Herr Kalbeck gives very cleverly his reasons for his alterations. He follows and explains Octavio's doings and movements on and off the stage, his emotions, his changing decisions up to the last of the recitative passages quoted, to which he now gives the following form: "Be cheered, Beloved! I have challenged the insolent knave today, tomorrow we meet." On the other hand he drops the first passage altogether.

I shall refrain from quoting all further lesser doubts, delicate points and elaborations which translators have taken pains over at these and other moments in the book with varying success. I shall omit likewise the analysis of the text and abstain from drawing special attention to the beauty of the music and refer the reader who is curious biographically to Otto Jahn's well-known work.

But I shall devote a short paragraph to the method of linguistic translation in general and to its application in particular.

In the translation into German of an Italian text fitted to the music the most outstanding difficulties are:

1. The reproduction of the euphony.
2. The imitation of that characteristic elastic metre which can make a trochee of a dactyl or vice versa according to whether the last syllable of a word is run on to the next word or separated from it. The following, taken from the original poem and intended as a five-foot iambic verse:

   Deh! vie / ni alla / fine / stra o mio / teso / ro

   can, after examination of the composition (Mozart's setting) run in the following manner:

   Deh / vie ni al / la fi / nestra o / mio te / so ro

   and would also be right thus:

   Deh / vieni / alla fi / nestra o / mio te / so ro

   Even greater difficulty arises for the translator if one and the same metrical foot of the composition is used twice alternately as trochee and dactyl.
3. The transcription of those phrases (especially in the *buffo* parts) for which the volubility of the Latin singers is calculated upon. In these sentences a load of consonants and difficult sounds (*Ku schuchs*, etc.) which delay the tongue must be avoided.
4. The employment of pure sounds on high notes and in coloratura passages.
5. Adapting the words and preserving their true sense in the subtleties of imitative music in places where the delay of a single syllable can produce disturbance.

Finally, in Nach-Rochlitz's German adaptation of the text of *Don Giovanni* two more instances are added:

(a) The controversy over many verses at the beginning of the opera which have become popular and the removal of which would lead the ordinary theatre-goer to lose his way, but the retention of which on the other hand cannot always be justified.

(b) The practical difficulties arising from the unwillingness of our singers to learn a new text.

It may be remarked, incidentally, in order to illustrate these short principles with an example, that the "Catalogue" aria presents difficulties of the third and fifth kind in particular to the translator. Care must be taken to select the separate, concise, telling phrases for which Mozart's music is written (all the quotations are from the arias in the second part): for example "e la grande maestosa", the phrase with which the music actually swings up to a climax and a majestic pause with which, up to now, Kalbeck has succeeded best (supported by Grandaur's diction).

Greatly splendid	Grosze prächtig
Proud and powerful	Stolz und mächtig
Grave	Gravitätisch
Majestic	Majestätisch

But against this Leporello's malicious remark:

Sua passion predominante
è la giovin principiante

which gives one the picture unmistakably as he slyly shuts one eye, means in approximate popular German prose: "Doch die junge Anfängerin war von jeher seine Schwäche", and Grandaur gives it the suitable interpretation:

Doch wofür er immer glühte
Ist der Jugend erste Blüte

Whilst Kalbeck's

Doch daneben
Junges Leben
Maien-blüte
Im Gemüte

is not drastic enough. At the end, on the other hand, "Voi
sapete quel che fa" where Mozart envelopes himself in a veil
of discretion in such an excellent way, Kalbeck, through the
literal truth of the translation "Nun Ihr wiszt ja, wie er's macht"
is the only one who is successful. As opposed to this, Grandaur's
transcription "Kennt ja selbst ihn ganz genau" misses distinction. Rietz quotes a capital old German parody of this
aria, a fragment of which can find a place here:

> Zwar die Blonden lobt er immer
> Als die feinsten Frauenzimmer
> Aber die mit dunklern Haaren
> Lässt er gleich wohl niemals fahren.
> Öfters fragt er: Ist sie dicke?
> Öfters noch: Ist sie auch flicke?
> Manchmal sucht er nach der Grössten,
> Doch die Kleinen sind die besten
> Auch die Alten muss ich fangen,
> Im Register mitzuprangen;
> Doch das meiste, was ich miete,
> Ist: die Jungfern in der Blüte.

My reason for continually coupling the names of Grandaur
and Kalbeck is that Kalbeck himself has defined the former
as "the last and most favoured of his predecessors", and because
Kalbeck's work, as he declares in his preface, developed
independently out of his revision of Grandaur's text. It is Kalbeck who has succeeded best in solving all the difficulties mentioned above. His success in striving for a flexible poetical form
related to the music deserves special notice and appreciation: a
form which recognises the metrical word as the natural support
of the metrical melody, and through the fullness of rhyme-
embellishment endeavours to re-introduce what the German
poem lacks in perceptible charm of timbre, in comparison
with the euphony of vocal richness in the Italian language. He
must be praised also for the transformation of Don Octavio,

which has already been mentioned with admiration. For the first of these two merits the Canzonetta, which Kalbeck has translated into German with special care, cannot be too highly valued and I will quote it as I cannot withhold the enjoyment of it from the reader:

Die Laute fleht: Erscheine,Du holde Kleine,
Vor Gram und Sehnsucht hier vergeht der Deine!
O, schenke Mitleid mir, erhör mein Werben!
Denn sonst, zu Füssen Dir, siehst Du mich sterben!

Vertraue süsse Kunde deinem Munde,
Dass von tödlicher Wunde mein Herz gesunde!
Du kannst nicht grausam sein, bei meinen Tränen,
Lass mich zu Dir hinein und stille mein Sehnen!

Before I turn to an important question, with which the essay under consideration will end, I will give a list of the editions and translations of *Don Giovanni*. This list lays claim to clearness rather than to completeness.

Mozart's original copy is in the possession of Frau Pauline Viardot-Garcia. According to the written copy belonging to the Stuttgart Court Theatre the score appeared for the first time in print in 1861 published by Breitkopf & Härtel and with Rochlitz's translation of the words.

This was engraved for the first time in 1840. After this, Peters published the accepted edition of the score in their edition. Gugler (published by Leuckart 1869) and Rietz (published by Breitkopf & Härtel 1871), each try to claim the honour of being the first publication according to Mozart's autograph. It seems that the work undertaken by Rietz, which was begun earlier, only achieved publication later. Both works are distinguished by extraordinary care and fidelity, but these qualities are particularly outstanding in the first one. Amongst the prominent musical editions, Gutmann's, which was prepared for the *Don Giovanni* Jubilee, must be mentioned with respect.[1]

Amongst the translations these may be mentioned here: *Der bestrafte Wollüstling oder der Krug geht so lange zum Wasser, bis er bricht* [E. G. Neefe, 1789]; *Die redende Statue* [Augsburg, 1790]; the translations written for the Berlin [1790] and Amsterdam [1794] productions; Rochlitz's [1801]; Kalkbrenner's bowdlerization for Paris [1805; see Rietz's foreword]; Sever's [1854]; Dr. W. Viol's [Breslau, Leuckart, 1858]; Bischoff's [1858]; A. v. Wolzogen's new adaptation with complete scenario published in *Die deutsche Schaubühne* [1860; No. 9]; (the reprint of Da Ponte's original text edited by Sonnleithner, 1865); Bitter's [1866]; Mode's [1868]; Gugler's [1869; based on Wolzogen's text]; T. Epstein's [1870]; Rietz's edition [1871]; Niese's [1874]; Grandaur's [1871, 1874 and 1882, published by Ackermann, Munich]; H. M. Schletterer's [*Don Juan* or *Der steinerne Gast*]; and, finally, Max Kalbeck's [1886, 1887].

I come now to a question which has agitated many musical minds, and occasioned much pondering by many scrupulous researchers. I mean the question of the authenticity of the trombones in the second Finale of *Don Giovanni*.

Here two of the most conscientious, most learned, and most authoritative men, Gugler and Rietz, who were absorbed in the same matter with equal industry and perseverance and who knew how to penetrate into the spirit of Mozart's works, stand opposite one another, for their opinions clash. Both have strong grounds for the defence of their belief and some admirable evidence and yet neither can oust the other. The reader will be left in no doubt of this if we give a summary of the evidence adduced by each.

[1] *Don Giovanni: Opera Buffa* in Two Acts by Lorenzo da Ponte. Freely transcribed by Max Kalbeck. Music by W. A. Mozart. Arranged for the piano from the original score with complete Secco Recitatives, by Joh. Nep. Fuchs (Vienna Albert J. Gutmann, Jubiläums Ausgabe). The latest and not the least important of these publications is the "Edition Modèle" of the score brought out for the Jubilee Celebrations by the Paris publisher Heugel.

Gugler's conclusions are as follows:

1. The trombones in the Finale are a later addition and were not present at the first performance in Prague.
2. The overcrowding generally, which follows, from the addition and the treatment of the trombones in particular, is not in accordance with Mozart's style of writing. More than this, it offends against his style, indeed against sensitive musical feeling altogether and, in some ways, so strongly that it is impossible to believe that the addition was Mozart's originally.
3. Should it be proved that the trombones were already there at the first performance in Vienna and that even with Mozart's knowledge they were crammed into the orchestra (by Süssmayr?) Mozart cannot have wished them to be there but merely put up with them indulgently and this would not alter the fact that the Finale has lost something thereby.

But so long as no such proof is brought forward, by far the most probable explanation is that the trombones were brought in after Mozart's death.

In the first Prague copy of the score, the trumpets and the kettledrums are written out as appendix to the second Finale, the trombones are not. If they had existed already their omission in the appendix would be unaccountable. If the Finale in Prague had no trombones this would be significant enough, quite apart from the consideration of the question of the authenticity, for if Mozart himself did put them in subsequently for the Vienna public he had not got them in mind at all in the original conception of his book. So much for Gugler's conclusions.

Rietz writes:

The trumpets, kettledrums and trombones are absent. With regard to the latter B. Gugler has published a very detailed investigation (*Allegemeine Musikalische Zeitung,*

1867, Nos. 1–3) the result of which he summarises in the following sentences. [Rietz here quotes Gugler's concluding sentences 1, 2 and 3, already quoted.]

My assurance given in No. 4 of the *Allegemeine Musikalische Zeitung*, 1867, immediately after the appearance of the treatise quoted, that in the years 1834 and 1836 at Hofrat Anton André's in Offenbach I have often seen and had in my hands the sheet with the part specially written for the trombones, is not, Gugler declares, sufficient evidence for the authenticity of the trombones and he does not give up the suspicion that Süszmeyer [*sic*] was the originator of them because it has been sufficiently substantiated that there was a great resemblance between Süszmeyer's [*sic*] and, Mozart's handwriting.

The arguments which Rietz brings forward now are of a purely artistic nature and although as such they are completely justifiable and of the kind which would obtain the concurrence of every good musician yet they are not positive enough and not founded enough on facts. It is striking that Rietz, in opposition to Gugler, is of the opinion that "the old Prague copy, so often mentioned, is a true copy of the autograph one, such as can only be done by a paid copyist *and contains the trombones*".

If we undertook an examination of these opinions of both authorities, we could reply first to Gugler's argument "that the treatment of the trombones is not in accordance with Mozart's style of writing", that what Mozart composed for the trombones gives much too small a choice for us to decide on his treatment of trombones generally or set up a rule about it.

His view that this treatment offends "against fine musical feeling altogether" is of a purely subjective nature and consequently cannot be decisive. Moreover the two statements about the Prague manuscript do not tally and the persistent representation of the similarity between Süssmayr's and Mozart's handwriting is not convincing.

But the opinion "that Mozart in the original conception of his work had not got the trombones in mind at all" can be disproved by the quotation of a simple fact through which may be found the solution of the trombone question altogether.

As is well known, two Adagio passages, with which the Commendatore's voice breaks into the free conversation between Don Giovanni and Leporello, are to be found inserted between the "Secco" recitative in the cemetery scene. Both these passages are accompanied by four oboes, two clarinets, two bassoons, the bass strings and three trombones.

Rietz and Gugler alike agree that the whole recitative together with the accompanied passages are missing in the autograph copy.

It is strange that it occurs to neither of them and to no one else to raise objections to these trombones or a doubt as to their authenticity. In this place they were found, with justification, to be quite right and at the commencement of this essay I have tried to point out in what a masterly manner their moving effect is imagined and calculated.

But is it not evident that in the employment of the trombones in this scene lies a striking proof that Mozart himself had thought of the trombones as a special characterisation of the apparition of the Commendatore? And is it not most obvious as an artistic consequence and correspondingly logical that they should always accompany this apparition and consequently return at the last?

Finally one could even quote a sentence of Gugler's which runs thus: "In the autograph copy there are no trombones: the trumpets and kettledrums are also missing from it", which joined with Rietz' assurance that the Prague copy contains the trombones shows a second favourable inference for the authenticity of the trombones.

As an Italian I must substantiate the sad fact of the disappearance of *Don Giovanni* from Italian repertoires. The ground for this may lie first of all in the fact that the capacity for good singing is dying out gradually (a great deal of this is necessary for *Don Giovanni*), and on the other side in the decline of simple feeling amongst the audience.

They find that the music is old-fashioned and childish. I find that taste is spoilt and the understanding enfeebled. The people there should be reminded of Lessing's confession which runs, though in other words: "I have learnt to perceive that if something does not please me in Homer, the blame does not lie with Homer but with me".

Schumann also says with truth: "Perhaps only a genius understands genius completely." And who knows how much there is in *Don Giovanni* that we are still not able to grasp and of which perhaps only a new genius will inform us?

But while waiting for him we must not grow weak. We must strive to seek for new enjoyment ourselves, continually increasing our stock of knowledge, ennobling our taste through the works and in the inexhaustible and sublime effect produced by the Master of Sound who, the best of his time, has done and lived enough for all times.

MOZART'S LIBRETTI*

THE German people, who with the greatest reverence for their geniuses easily become familiar with them, deny the excellence of Mozart libretti and speak of "bad" texts although:

1. Mozart's infallible instinct for choice remains unquestioned.
2. The characters in his pieces are alive and have not dated.
3. Quotations from his operas have become proverbial.
4. The three types—Drama, Comedy, Symbolic Action— appear finally established in his work.
5. Goethe showed his estimation of *The Magic Flute* as a poem by writing a continuation of it.

* Written in Berlin at the end of 1920, published in *Von der Einheit der Musik*.

6. Managers do not shrink from presenting the originals of the Mozart libretti as spoken drama—among them literary and dramatic masterpieces such as Tirso de Molina's *Don Juan Tenorio* (*El Burlador de Sevilla*), Beaumarchais' *La folle journée* (*Le Mariage de Figaro*).

In spite of all this, the German art aestheticists, critics and historians speak against Mozart's libretti. On the other hand Grillparzer says finely (1822):

If the text of the opera *Don Giovanni* which Mozart has composed, is taken directly and without any doubt from Molière's *Festin de pierre*, one cannot do enough justice to the art of the transcriber, to his knowledge of that which belongs to the opera, and to his deep insight into the essence of music. That transcription is a model for all similar transcriptions and Kind would have done well to take it as an example for his *Freischütz*.

VII

BEETHOVEN

WHAT DID BEETHOVEN GIVE US?*

IT has often happened to me while playing a Mozart score that my listener has cried out: "That is quite Beethovenish." The reverse has happened at certain moments during a piece by Beethoven and my young friend has remarked: "That is really quite Mozartian." The first remark accompanied by respectful astonishment, the second by an indulgent smile. My listener in both instances overlooked the fact that Mozart where he was found "Beethovenish" was important and original, whereas Beethoven when he recalled Mozart was unimportant and merely borrowing from him. In other words: Mozart can at times strike the note which in Beethoven fills our generation with awe. But Beethoven cannot reach Mozart where he floats in front of him. He has pushed Mozart into the background so much that to quote an opus number of Beethoven's inaccurately makes my generation blush, but it need have no shame if a concerto or opera by Mozart is not known at all. Moritz Heimann in one of his short stories, makes a German poet in Italy say: "They have not got a Beethoven." You might speak of "the divine Rossini". You can also speak of "the divine Mozart". But you cannot say "the divine Beethoven". That does not sound right. You must say "the human Beethoven". It is in this way that he is great. Apart from the fact that there has never been an example of every particular kind of phenomenon in every country. None but England has a Shakespeare, none but Italy has a Michelangelo, only Spain possesses a

* Written in Berlin, 20th November 1920. Published for the first time in *Von der Einheit der Musik*, 1922.

Cervantes. Yet what Heimann says gives the key to a particular problem, namely: with Beethoven humanity enters into music for the first time as the principal argument in the place of interplay of figures.

At once the question arises as to whether this signifies a gain, an advance for music; whether it is the task of music to be human instead of remaining pure sound and beautiful form—Beethoven's heart was great and pure and it felt for humanity, it suffered for it and beat for it. That is chiefly an affair of sentiment, of feeling; Beethoven, the artist, had to be formed; and his proverbial struggles may be nothing else than the difficult endeavour to put human strivings (which, at times, mean things beyond the sphere of music) into musical forms. In this he succeeded, frequently succeeded—but the music thereby was conducted into another region than that which it had inhabited hitherto. Through Beethoven we have accustomed ourselves to thinking of this region as the only one compatible with music. We think of this as its own territory—and we shall uphold this principle for some time yet.

Beethoven's human ideals are high and pure. They are the ideals of the just at all times and in all zones, the impulse towards freedom, salvation through love, the brotherhood of all men. Liberty, equality, fraternity: Beethoven is a product of 1793, and he was the first great democrat in music. He wished art to be serious and life cheerful; his work is full of depression, for life is not cheerful; with noble yearning towards this realisation he is always up in arms under affliction, furious and rebellious. "Non per portas, per muros, per muros"—"Must it be? It must be"—"Oh, friends not tones such as these"—"Destiny knocks at the door." These are some of the mottoes which characterise Beethoven—constant defiance, desire for the resolution of dissonance, and running his head against a wall. The heart is big, the sentiment golden, the head is not correspondingly disciplined. It was on this account that Goethe had misgivings about Beethoven's art, misgivings on which people readily put an interpretation unfavourable to Goethe and yet—if one puts Goethe's comprehensive understanding for Mozart in the scales—this should have given cause for reflection sooner. But nothing will be discussed about Beethoven for another half century.

For his contemporaries, Beethoven was chiefly an amazing curiosity—a concert at which the fifth and sixth Symphonies and the G major Pianoforte Concerto were performed for the first time left the public quite unmoved. *Fidelio* was a fiasco twice, the Violin Concerto was described as being unmelodious and forced. But soon the situation changed, the reaction set in and continued for two generations.

Quite spontaneously—very different from Wagner's case—a militant priesthood arose and from now on Beethoven's increasingly successful work was guarded as the symbol of musical humanity. Throughout two generations it was the aim of ambitious composers to write their nine symphonies. Brahms, Bruckner, Mahler, were all filled with the monomania of writing their own nine symphonies; notwithstanding the fact that in art it is not the line you take but the gift you possess which is the deciding factor, however much you may wish they were the same thing. "One follows a great example most faithfully by turning away from it", I said once, and by that I meant that an example is great because it creates a *new* type. If the type is repeated nothing new is created and the idea of an example is destroyed. Beethoven's work aroused in his successors the ambition to put significance and depth into their work and to compose on a cyclopean scale; the measurement of width and of means piled up chronologically. Yet Haydn finished symphonies with the same ease and joy as he wrote down a piano minuet. Since Beethoven, everything must be "powerful": even with his first composition a young composer wishes to surpass in weight everything that has been written previously. The joy which Beethoven sings about fanatically, from the ardent desire for what was missing, is out of sight. In former times, the listener greeted the preparations for a musical performance with a smile of pleasant expectation but now one sits down to listen with closed eyes and hopeless earnestness. A piece which turns out to be cheerful and short, however beautiful and masterly it may be, will be classed as a work of second rank. Art declines into handicraft if it is without the quality of human vibration. But what is *not* human? Without exception everything that is felt and undertaken by human beings is human. Art—that is why it is art and not life itself—has the privilege of being able to choose what is to its taste. Pictorial art chooses from the abundance of visible things, musical art from the whole scale of human impressions. On the other hand it has the right to push aside what does not belong to it, what lives outside itself, and I feel that, however violently a composer may be filled with such themes, matters of social tendency and movements of propaganda belong, above all, to this category! It is in this way that a poet becomes a popular speaker. Defiance, resentment, reconciliation, lay nearest to Beethoven's nature; in this he was faultlessly *sincere*; and with this knowledge we obtain the first important answer to the question: "What does Beethoven signify to the people of today?" *Sincerity* is one of the absolute necessities for the existence and activity of creation.

In this Beethoven has certainly set us a high standard in that his rigorous sincerity led him instinctively to spheres which are quite his own. But we can observe this standard in all truly important people from Dante to—yes, to Beethoven; and so compelling is the strength of sincerity, that through it less important composers also reach a high rank and have a lasting value—presuming that the necessary skill, feeling, and power of imagination are there. Among later-comers, because they come into one's mind of their own accord, I may mention Weber, Chopin, Bizet.

A second motive with Beethoven that the youth of the present day might take to heart is the *subservience of virtuosity to the Idea*. He controls orchestra and counterpoint with preeminence and yet we never think of him first and foremost as an "orchestrator" or a "contrapuntalist". The special label of "symphonic composer" has been affixed to him, it is true, yet this is a convention, like every other label. The Hammerklavier Sonata and the C sharp minor String Quartet certainly outweigh the symphonies in content; in fact with Beethoven it is rather a matter of indifference what medium conveys his thought to us. As "specialists" his predecessors have surpassed him: Bach's harmony is more daring and richer, Mozart's orchestration is more balanced, Haydn's quartet writing is purer and more transparent. That is because Beethoven's impetuosity often allowed him to reach beyond the comfortable possibilities of the instrument or voices; whereby "risk" came into the performance which is dangerous to euphony. But in return he compelled and helped instrumentalists and orchestras to obtain greater powers of execution; power over difficulties and power of endurance and thought. The master does not always appear in restraint, but it is precisely in expansion that his mastery shows, the moment he controls it.

Unfortunately this gesture of Beethoven's has been eagerly taken up subsequently. Over-emphasis, indulged in for its own sake, leads to decadence because it widens the gap between content and display. In the "Eroica", the third horn added to the customary pair caused sensation and provoked reflection, nevertheless the employment of it is justified and convincingly carried out. What similar right is there to the eight and twelve horns in many present-day scores?

To suffer for humanity is extremely "human", commands respect and is worthy of thanks and love—but the "Divine" which neither knows nor awakens any doubt and which allows all suffering to be forgotten is worthy of adoration.

FROM THE ZÜRICH PROGRAMMES
BEETHOVEN*

THE same decisive revolutionary step which Beethoven made

* Written in Zürich, 1915.

in symphonic forms, the Master also accomplished in expansion form in compositions for the pianoforte.

A greater transformation has not taken place in the history of music, than from the Sonata of Haydn and Mozart to the Sonata "for the Hammerklavier". Beethoven created the modern grand piano through his technique, by making the best use of higher, lower and wider positions on the keyboard, by the use of pedals and by the improvement and enrichment of the sound.

The sonata served him for this as a natural form of expression, as on the other hand the fugue had been, as a matter of course, Bach's form of expression.

With Beethoven the musical content is the initial impetus; in spite of all instrumental improvements the "pianoforte" itself is only a suitable tool which enables the music to be played and its meaning to be communicated.

This is principally shown in his later compositions when his creative power was most mature; the pianoforte technique is not subordinate but seems placed in perfect relationship to the mind, while the middle period of Beethoven's creation inclines rather towards the accentuation of external brilliance.

For this reason (and because one may assume that the earlier works are better known), Beethoven's latest works have been chosen for this Beethoven concert, including the Bagatelles op. 126, the Sonata op. 111, inward turning and rich in sound, and the most powerful composition for the pianoforte of all time, the Sonata op. 106 known as the "Hammerklavier".

BEETHOVEN AND MUSICAL HUMOUR*

HUMOUR in Beethoven is commended. It is said—so German writings inform me—that humour is the joke behind which seriousness is hidden (inverted irony). Beethoven is un-

* This comes from the handwritten posthumous works of Busoni, previously unpublished.

deniably serious and just as undeniably he is at times disposed
to joke. But he does not apply the joke to things about which
he is serious. There are, for Beethoven, things "about which
one does not joke". The ability to do this requires someone
whose habit it is to be more cheerful, the habit of a sceptic.

It would not be in accordance with Beethoven's views to
look at a king from a humorous point of view. In a king he
sees the "tyrant", his democratic feeling rises and it is all over
with the good mood. In the idea of a king he only sees a threat
to human freedom. A ridiculous, good-hearted king does not
agree with his conception of one; His Majesty, in a fairy-tale,
or a Serene Highness, do not fit into Beethoven's circle of
ideas. A philosophic superiority is required for that, which
enters tyranny and freedom in the book of history as social
events of equal value; both equally great or both equally unimportant. It is this view of earthly proceedings that produces
the humorist, and the more genuine he is the more indifferent
he remains, and the fewer "views" he has about anything.
Everybody would be obliged to deny that the pathetic, iras-
cible Beethoven could be called a humorist in this sense. In
this Offenbach, a descendant of Shakespeare, is superior to him.
I am thinking of Pyramus and Thisbe, of Troilus and Cressida.

With Beethoven it goes so far that he is unable to perceive
the underlying seriousness in other people's humour. It is said
that he dismissed Mozart's libretti for *Figaro* and *Don Giovanni*
as "frivolous". He would not admit that Shakespeare's fool is
the serious person in the play, the character who speaks the
truth; one of mankind's most serious appointments. As with
his idea of power, his conception of every kind of humour is
one of helplessness, something requiring protection. The picture of poverty fills him with pain and with sympathy for the
suffering caused by injustice. And yet there are beggars who
are also comical, indeed there is "tragi-comedy", unknown to
Beethoven, in all situations and ranks of life. The origins of
Beethoven's jovial moments are unpretentious and harmless,
they bear on things that, for him, are quite insignificant. It

must be affirmed that in the music these moments are also not there without metaphorical significance, the essence of music having no purpose. The origin of Beethoven's alleged humour springs from Haydn—that is to say, it is jocose and conversational, or called forth by mockery (for example, his amusement over Mälzel's metronome) really *buon umore* but not humorous. I said that humour in music would be unthinkable without metaphorical meaning. Something like this: in Berlioz' *Faust*, when a fugue is started on the word "Amen", the effect is comical because this "Amen" is sung by intoxicated students in a wine cellar, added to this it has to do with the death of a rat. By itself this fugue is not at all funny—it is only funny through the strength of a series of thought associations: Religion—poisoned rat—drunkenness. The fugue is certainly a solid piece of music that would not mar a fairly good mass. But Beethoven would never have undertaken anything like a parody on the word "Amen". The word is sacred for him. "There are things about which one does not joke."

And without association of ideas, to what extent can music be much more humorous than that?

We maintain that it is impossible.

There are, however, certain formulas that pass for humour. Short staccato themes, surprisingly deceptive cadences in the place of the expected tonic; but—particularly the solo bassoon in leaps in the lowest register (when it does not wish to imitate piccolo flutes at all), these are called "musical humour"; a typically symbolic little piece of this kind is the quotation, never refused, from the song "O du mein lieber Augustin", a popular orchestral witticism which makes everybody laugh. During the interval it was the custom with the Boston Symphony Orchestra to play a little piece ending on the seventh bar. People found it "awfully funny" that the eighth bar was left out. Funny it is—but not humorous, for humour presupposes a literary thought which is not to be found in purely instrumental music. Bandmasters cultivate such jokes as the one above and in garden restaurants they will be understood, enjoyed and applauded by the simplest audience. If these small jokes were something belonging to humour they would not be applauded, because in the highest social scale what is humorous is taken as a species of joviality.

How could Beethoven be a humorist when he was not able to smile at seriousness and the libretto of *Figaro* annoyed him? Caricatures are not drawn on the monument to a hero; that stone is sacred. But Beethoven would not have treated the Berlin Siegesallee with irony either, but he should certainly have grumbled for two reasons. Among human beings he is of greater size than the average but not a human being over human beings, that is (as Heine differentiates) a Nazarene and not a Greek. The crown he wears is a crown of thorns which lacerates his forehead.

How could humour unfold in one so afflicted?

VIII

LISZT

FROM THE ZÜRICH PROGRAMMES
LISZT*

THE Grand Duke Karl Alexander of Weimar, when he was
eighty years of age, once said to me: "Liszt was what a Prince
should be." He was Prince, artist, and already in his lifetime a
legend. His disposition was princely, his appearance and his
carriage. The happy combination of gifts, intelligence, per-
serverance and idealism marked him as an artist and as such he
possessed all the distinguishing marks of greatness; the universality of his art, the three creative periods, the seeking up to the
last. The riddle of his giftedness, the magic of his playing, the
magnetic impression produced by his art, invested Liszt with
the title "legendary".

His aims are ascent, ennoblement, and liberation. Only one
who is exalted strives to ascend, only one who is noble strives
for nobility, only a master of freedom can bestow freedom.

He has become the symbol of the pianoforte, which he
lifted to a princely position in order that it might be worthy
of himself.

OPEN LETTER ABOUT LISZT †

Dear Mr. Kastner,

I have received your welcome greeting and read it with deep
gratitude. It came in the middle of renewed impressions.
Yesterday evening I read the *Tagebuch* in which you refer to
me in a flattering manner. . . .

* Written in Zürich, April 1916, for the Zürich programmes.
† Letter to *Das Tagebuch*.

138

I observe with astonishment from your article that you put Liszt aside with a light gesture. . . . I know Liszt's weaknesses but I do not misjudge his strength. We are all descended from him radically, without excepting Wagner, and we owe to him the lesser things that we can do. César Franck, Richard Strauss, Debussy, the penultimate Russians, are all branches of his tree, therefore in one and the same sentence in which Respighi is extolled, Liszt should not be rejected. No later-comers have succeeded with a *Faust* Symphony, a *Heilige Elisabeth* and a *Christus. Les jeux d'eau* still remains today the model for all musical fountains which have flowed since then. . . . In any case, if you have good reasons for your rejection you should state them, and not presume without further ceremony, that every reader knows them and every musician agrees with you. I, personally, do not see what Liszt has spoilt in Schubert's *Wandererfantasie.* On the contrary, I have been obliged to recognise how helpfully Liszt shows the way over certain "stretches" in the original. Also, it can compromise no pianist if he shows himself to be of the same opinion as Liszt, otherwise it must follow that he excels Liszt as musician and pianist. Such a pianist, up to now, is not known to me. I am myself respectfully conscious of the distance which separates me from his greatness. I beg you, therefore, to forgive me for expressing my view on this subject.

Yours,

with warmest regards,

F. B.

BIBLIOGRAPHICAL AND CRITICAL STUDY DRAWN UP AS A FOUNDATION TO THE PROPOSED COLLECTED EDITION OF LISZT'S PIANOFORTE WORKS *

THE compiling of a chronological, bibliographical and complete collection of Liszt's pianoforte works is one of the most

* Published in the *Allegemeine Musik-Zeitung,* XXII, 1900, and in *Von der Einheit der Musik,* 1922.

difficult undertakings of the kind, in spite of the fact that only fourteen years have elapsed since Liszt's death and people are alive to testify to the origin and publication of many of these works. The complication is caused, I consider, by mistakes in the opus numbers, by the unusually large numbers of publishers, by the existence of two, three and even more versions of one and the same piece (and in certain cases the publication of the same pieces under two different names), and finally by the disappearance of every earlier edition from the market as soon as a new one appeared.

I have succeeded, after many years of research, in obtaining a certain insight into these matters and I now impart the result of my studies. These notes are neither complete nor exhaustive and they will only indicate the direction which will have to be taken in compiling a collected edition. Therefore I shall quote only those works for the piano which have experienced more than one revision, as the details of these manifold versions cannot be understood clearly from any catalogue. And as a man who keeps things in order can find what he seeks even in the dark, I set to work systematically and divided my—or rather Liszt's—work into large groups.

First of all the voluminous serial works: 1. *Etuden.* 2. *Années de Pèlerinage.* 3. *Ungarische Rhapsodien.* 4. *Harmonies poétiques et religieuses*; three *Valses Caprices*, single piano pieces, *Apparitions.* 5. Schubert. 6. Opera Fantasies—finally and at the same time as a key to the foregoing the works provided with opus numbering up to 13.

My review will elucidate this general arrangement which is still veiled in obscurity.

Studies

There are twenty-four altogether. First, the twelve Great Studies: They appear under op. 1, edited by Hofmeister, and a second edition by Haslinger 1839.[1]

[1] *Vingt-quatre Grandes Études*, Livraison 1 and 2 (the projected Studies 13-24 are left out).

Eleven of the studies of this edition originated in the first, but they underwent such a transformation here that Schumann, for example, did not recognise the origin of the sixth and eighth, and referred to them, as well as to the seventh, as "quite new". In this second edition the separate pieces are still without titles. The seventh study is really new in spite of the fact that the introductory bars are borrowed from an earlier work, the Impromptu, op. 3. Between this edition and the third and final one (Breitkopf & Hartel), an altered version of the fourth study appeared (Schlesinger, Paris). For the first time it has the title "Mazeppa" and the dedication "à Victor Hugo". The dedication and two additional lines of introduction (the arpeggio chords) were printed from a special plate, the notes in a facsimile of Liszt's handwriting.

The content of the second page is the same as in the first edition. At the end the fall and the recovery of the hero (recitative and D major fanfare) are new; the recitative is still in embryo. In a new impression of this version (published by Haslinger Wittwe) the introduction on the first plate is engraved for the first time and, including the title and dedication, is the same as the French edition. The third edition of the studies is certainly more playable and as compositions they are more rounded off than in the second edition, but it leaves out many strokes of genius, and many musical beauties of the earlier version are missing; for example, the unity of the seventh study ("Eroica") and the romantic introduction to the twelfth ("Chasse-neige").

Secondly, the six Paganini Studies. They are extant in two editions, the first published by Haslinger, the second by Breitkopf & Härtel. In the first edition there are already two versions of the fourth of these studies, in E major. In going back to the original source of these studies the *Fantaisie sur la Clochette de Paganini*, op. 2, must certainly be mentioned. The two editions of the Paganini studies stand in the same relationship to each other as the second and third editions of the twelve Great Studies and the dates of their publication probably coincided also.

Thirdly, under the title of *Morceau de Salon: Étude de Perfectionnement*, which later became transformed into *Ab-Irato*,[1] two editions of a single study were published by Schlesinger.

The remaining studies: *Trois Études de Concert* (Kistner) and those composed for the Lebert & Stark school "Waldesrauschen" and "Gnomenreigen", did not, I believe, undergo a single alteration.

Années de Pèlerinage

They are, as is well known, divided into three years, a set to each year; the title of the first set *Switzerland* and the other two *Italy*.[2]

But we are concerned here with the first two only, for the third set is a later and not, I think, a revised work. The origin of *Switzerland* may be traced to a pianoforte work *Fantaisies romantiques sur deux airs suisses* published with two other compositions by Haslinger and Hofmeister.[3] This piece is noteworthy on account of the directions to the executant which leave no doubt about the interpretation of any note, and also on account of the first appearance of the poetic and musical themes "Le mal du pays". *Switzerland's* second line of descent was from a work of a not much later date—*Trois airs suisses*, op. 10, which, besides being published by the original publishers, the Stammverlegern, also saw the light in Basle (Kahn published it recently in a new edition). It was incorporated shortly after its first appearance in a voluminous work *Album d'un Voyageur* which is the real forerunner of the first collection of the *Années de Pèlerinage*. The *Album* is in three

[1] With the concluding sentence: "Grande Étude de Perfectionnement de la Méthode des Méthodes"; also on the first page of notation is printed "Called *Étude de Salon*". Besides the fact that none of the many titles is specially suitable, it is not worth so many names.

[2] The third year has no name really but the more important half of it—according to its content—refers to Rome (1922).

[3] The first pianoforte compositions by Liszt were published usually at the same time by Haslinger in Austria, Hofmeister in Germany, Schlesinger in France and Ricordi in Italy.

parts: *Impressions et Poésies, Fleurs mélodiques des Alpes,* and *Paraphrases.* The first part contains: 1. "Lyon", allegro eroica. 2. "Le lac de Wallenstaedt—au Bord d'une Source". 3. "Les Cloches de * * * (Genève—observe how the stars conceal the name; a characteristic of those romantic times). 4. "Vallée d'Obermann".[1] 5. "La Chapelle de Guillaume Tell". 6. "Psaume de l'église de Genève." The second part, *Fleurs Mélodiques,* consists of nine pieces on Swiss Melodies without name. The three pieces *Paraphrases* are the same in content as those of op. 10. So much for *Switzerland.*

The set for the second year entitled *Italy* has no other model among Liszt's earlier works as far as I know, except the three sonnets of Petrarch which were published by Haslinger at the same time both as songs and for piano alone.[2] These six attractive octavo sheets decorated in the taste of the period have a title in Italian. The Swiss and Italian pieces in the earliest editions both as compositions and pianistically are very different from the final well-known versions. Numbers one and six in the first part of the *Album* are withdrawn from the later collection.

Hungarian Rhapsodies

When Liszt began to publish this, his most popular work, with the title *Magyar Dallók* (Hungarian Folk Songs) with Haslinger, his only idea was to record the national airs of his native country in order to preserve them for his people and to communicate them to other countries. But the task grew under his hand. The form of the sixth in the first book (in G minor) with its contrasting middle movement and the two variations of the principal motive makes a bridge to the Rhapsody, a name which was used from the fifth book onwards. Although

[1] With reference to the book *Obermann* by Sénancour, a collection of philosophical, romantic letters about Nature.

[2] Whether *Italie* exists as the second year of *Album d'un Voyageur* I am not able to say, for I have never seen such a volume. But that it had been planned is to be inferred from the fact that "Première Année Suisse" is to be read on the title page of the *Album.*

Haslinger's catalogue only lists four books of this work, from an old lending library catalogue of Roszavólgyi, to be seen in Pesth, it seems to have been continued up to the tenth. In any case the ninth, which came into my possession, is extant.

The exact connection between the seventeen numbers of the numbered collection and the present edition of the Hungarian Rhapsodies, could only be shown by musical examples that cannot be given here. However, I will try to trace a plan of the development of the Rhapsody now called the sixth in order that the reader may get an idea of this very intricate connection. The first sketch of the first two themes of the Rhapsody is to be found in the fourth and fifth of the seventeenth above-mentioned numbers of the earliest edition. I say "sketch" expressly, for the version lacks all pianistic embellishment and all the material necessary for a composition. The now famous octave-stretta of the Sixth Rhapsody appears for the first time as coda of No. 11. We must suppose that Liszt liked to play these three fragments in succession publicly and that he did so with popular success, for they were soon published in Paris as an independent volume by different publishers with the title *Trois Mélodies Hongroises*. Nothing is changed in this edition: only a modulating transition passage is inserted before the stretta. We must now suppose further that in the course of his repeated performances of this piece, half following a mood and half a definite design, and the natural artistic impulse towards variety, Liszt gradually enriched and adorned the composition, so that it became strikingly different from the original edition.

The first part has a brilliant kind of resonance found in cadenzas: the modulating transition passage has become a little technical problem. These changes and the probable demands of the public called for a new edition from composer and publisher. It was the third and was published by Haslinger Wittwe with the title *Ungarische National-Melodien*. Nevertheless this was and is (even in present-day conditions) considered to be so difficult that a simplified version had to be made for the great amateur public. It forms part of a collection of compositions which were published by Haslinger Wittwe with the collective title: *Neuigkeiten für das Pianoforte im eleganten Stile*. Later when Liszt finally undertook the revision of his complete piano works this piece took its place amongst the Hungarian Rhapsodies as the sixth. A long theme in B flat minor, one of the most beautiful of the Hungarian style, takes the place of the modulating transition passage. This final version is therefore the fifth version of one and the same piece, a fact which compels our admiration as much as it places us in confusion. The circumstances connecting the editions of the *Rákóczy* March, two different versions of which are found in the sixth volume of the earliest collection, are not very different. An *Édition Populaire* of the same march was published by Kistner: also an arrangement of the orchestral score by Schubert. Finally, in the new collection, the *Rákóczy* March appears as the Fifteenth Rhapsody and it has a different setting again from the four previous versions. In conclusion, the first separate edition of the *Pesther Carneval* must be mentioned, as it became the ninth Rhapsody later.

Truly Bach is the Alpha of pianoforte composition and Liszt the Omega. If with Liszt the atmosphere and content are less intensive, the sound and the magic are all the more impressive and effective. For Liszt's characteristic power lies in the expression of two points of feeling—the diabolic and catholic. They have never been brought together more harshly but also never more happily than in the last movement of the *Faust* Symphony. As opposed to this, the purely human feeling of passion, love, humour and the heart make a less convincing effect, yet a worldly versatility of form even makes these understandable and transitorily credible.

Harmonies Poétiques et Religieuses—Trois Valses Caprices—Single Piano Pieces—Apparitions

In Liszt's later years his pianoforte compositions gain in transparency and playableness but he loses his youthful daring.

The antitheses prevail in the youthful and the old Liszt—
Experiment—Routine, Improvisation—Manner. Not that the
later works are lacking altogether in inspiration and happy
ideas on that account, but the early and late periods of his compositions are characterised rather strongly with them perhaps.
The more polished Liszt of sixty or seventy years did not
achieve again the twilight charm of the improvised ecstasy
found in the first *Harmonies poétiques et religieuses*, the *Apparitions* and the introduction to the *Fantaisie sur la Clochette*. His
process of development is the opposite of Beethoven's. The
latter advanced from the limitations of the master to the
boundlessness of Nature—Liszt from free man of Nature to the
Master who controls the form but who does not step outside
it. Beautiful, solemn, and of charming timbre is the tenth of
Liszt's numbered pianoforte works (Volume VII) which has
the title *Harmonies poétiques et religieuses*. But it is scarcely so
direct in feeling as the first model bearing this name. This—the
first setting of the later *Pensée des Morts*—was published by
Schlesinger in Paris and by Hofmeister in Leipzig as a
separate piece. Nothing more suitable could be hit upon than
these words borrowed from the poet Lamartine which open
the introduction: "Ces vers ne s'adressent qu'à un petit nom-
bre" ("These lines are addressed to a few only").

A small serial work, *Trois Valses Caprices,* has also its bibliographical antecedents. The first of the waltzes, "Valse de
Bravoure", appeared under the opus no. 6—published by
Hofmeister & Schlesinger and Ricordi & Haslinger, as were
most of the first compositions. The second, "Valse Mélan-
colique", was likewise published separately by Haslinger but
first of all appeared as an *Albumblatt* (by Frieze in Leipzig in a
volume which also contains things by other composers) and
does no more than give the principal ideas within the compass
of a printed page. The third waltz, "Valse à Capriccio sur deux
motifs de Lucia et Parisina", published by Haslinger & Ricordi,
was the most important of the three in the first edition, but in
the later and simplified version "La Valse de Bravoure" takes

precedence over the other two. Ricordi also brought out an edition of the third waltz which in the setting corresponds to the first waltz and in one "stretch" it corresponds to the second waltz, so that it might be said that it is a question of three editions with this piece also. When published together the three took the title of the last and are called *Valses Caprices*. They form a vivacious and elegant work as pleasing to the pianist as to the listener, but unfortunately it is seldom played.

Apparitions, already mentioned, are composed in a more intimate, deeper and more serious spirit. They originate from three pieces. The first, *senza lentezza quasi allegretto*, written when the rays of the sinking sun were still shining on the youthful Liszt, cannot—as regards the impression produced and the content—be translated into words. It is romantic, enthusiastic and philosophic, and possesses that breath of Nature which is arrested with so much difficulty in art and so seldom. The second, more ingenuous and merely inscribed *vivamente*, is a capricious, almost "speaking" piece belonging to that kind of subjective impressionism which Schumann attempted and succeeded with in his earlier works, only he spoke as a German to Germans whereas Liszt spoke as a cosmopolitan to all people of culture and fine feeling. The third piece has no title in the French edition, but in the German edition is called, in French, "Fantaisie sur une valse de François Schubert". Even the first directions for execution: *molto agitato ed appassionato vibrante delirando senza tempo, precipitato*, which are followed, for example, not less significantly by: *quasi improvisato, avec coquetterie, religiosamente, con gioia*, can scarcely give an idea of the ecstatic, untamed, nervous atmosphere of this piece which, in spite of all incompleteness and arbitrariness, takes an exceptional place in the literature of the pianoforte.

The *Consolations* and the *Liebesträume* also belong to the class of all the "smaller serial works" already quoted. It is enough to mention them here.

I must confine myself also to naming only those of the scattered separate piano pieces which have two different set-

tings for that, I repeat, is the principal aim of these notes. The
titles in the first and second editions are as follows:

First Edition	Second Edition
Co Aoben[1]	*Le Rossignol* (First number of the two Russian melodies)
Gaudeamus	*Gaudeamus*
La Romanesca	*La Romanesca*
Élégie du Prince Louis Ferdinand	*Élégie, etc.*
Feuille d'Album	*Die Zelle in Nonnenworth*
Petite Valse favorite (Such a name exists, is it the original?)	*Valse impromptu*
Chant de Croise (Paris, with Meissonnier)	*Erste Ballade*
Galop Chromatique, op. 13	*Galop Chromatique*
Second *Marche Hongroise* (*Ungarischer Sturmmarsch*)	*Ungarischer Sturmmarsch*

Schubert

A special section must be given to the large part devoted by
Liszt to Schubert's compositions. These transcriptions made
Liszt popular in another way and with deeper effect than
through the Rhapsodies. With the Hungarian Melodies he
bewitched the listeners, with Schubert he enchanted them.
Instead of being conquered they surrendered. He delighted
society with the Rhapsodies; with the *Müller Lieder*, the
Schwanengesang and the *Winterreise* he won the people,
especially the German people.

No work, from the compositions of Beethoven and Hummel
to those of our time, shows more decidedly and completely
how the piano has been transformed. If we look at it in this way
we can to some extent form some conception of the mysterious
and magic impression made by Liszt's performance of these
transcriptions in his own day and in Schubert's own town.

[1] The title of this piece composed on a Russian melody was "Die
Nachtigall". Instead of printing one word in Russian characters the printer
printed two words in Latin characters.

The first experiment that Liszt made with Schubert's songs was the transcription of four of them, published in one volume and dedicated to the Ladies of Vienna.[1]

It is entitled *Hommage aux dames de Vienne*, and contains the following songs: "Ständchen", "Die Post", "Lob der Thränen" and "Die Rose".

Just as seeds sown in the soil disappear with the sprouting of the plant, so every trace of the existence of this work vanished as soon as the series of twenty-six numbers of the *Schwanengesang* and the *Winterreise* made its appearance, except for the title which is to be found in Haslinger's catalogue and index; in fact this is the only original edition I could neither obtain nor even look at at any time.[2]

The fact that Liszt, contrary to his custom, never revised this work for a second edition, with the exception of "Die Forelle" and the *Soirées de Vienne*, is a significant proof of the immediate success of the work.[3]

At the first attempt the Schubert transcriptions achieved that irrevocable perfection which belongs to organic functions only. The transcriber's enthusiasm for, as it were, the newly discovered Schubert, floats like a sun mist at dawn over Schubert's springlike melodies. How right the Master was not to banish it through the clearer unbroken light of his midday beams.

In order of importance the Schubert-Liszt collection for pianoforte appears as follows:

1. *Schwanengesang*, *Winterreise*, Lob der Thränen, Die Rose. Altogether twenty-six numbers in a single octavo volume published by Haslinger (newly printed by Schlesinger).

---

[1] Whether this title was inspired by Schubert's op. 67 *Hommage aux belles Viennoises* (Damenländler) is uncertain.

[2] In the meantime I have found this also (1922).

[3] In my possession is a separate French publication of the "Ave Maria" to which, instead of the back cover, a piece of manuscript paper is fastened. This contains the last printed page of a recitative, fantastical ending to this "Ave Maria", unknown to me, which originated unmistakably from Liszt. I shall be grateful if any kind and competent person can give me an explanation of this.

2. Six *Müller Lieder* (Diabelli).

3. Twelve *Lieder* in twelve numbers (Diabelli).

4. Six *Mélodies de Schubert* (Schlesinger). "Die Forelle" also amongst them in the second version.

5. *Geistlicher Lieder*, four numbers.

6. Three *Märsche*.

7. *Mélodies hongroises*, three numbers.

8. The same, "an easier setting".

9. *Soirées de Vienne*, nine numbers in two revisions.

10. *Fantasie*, op. 15 for piano and orchestra, "symphonically transcribed". Also arranged for pianoforte alone in Liszt's collection of Schubert's pianoforte compositions.

Fantasies on Italian and French Operas

Here the theatrical and dramatic impulse is added to all Liszt's earlier pianoforte achievements. The means, to their furthest limits, are used to the best advantage—for example, the compass of the keyboard, big chords, bravura playing, heightening of the contrasts for the expression of pathos, greatest freedom and subjectivity in the conception; these are the most remarkable characteristics of this side of his creative power.

But besides these "decorative painting" methods, it is the ennoblement, the elevation and aggrandisement of the musical content which give the Fantasies a high artistic rank. Anyone who has listened to or played the Finale of "Lucrezia", the middle section in B major in "Norma", or the slow movement in "Sonnambula", without being moved has not yet arrived at Liszt. Perhaps a romantic vein is required in order to enjoy this music completely, in any case blood which is not too purely Germanic. The influence of Italian melody on Liszt's own creative power was never extinguished and to my mind the Fantasies are important in this respect also. They open the way to the understanding of Liszt's melody formation and of the pathos peculiar to it, the two points which have made the approach to Liszt more difficult for the German people and even prevented it. In so far as the form and style are concerned I consider "Die Puritaner", op. 7, as the perfect model for all later *paraphrases*; the timbre, however, is to be found already in the "Fantaisie sur la Niobe", op. 5. The "Niobe", "Sonnambula", "Hugenotten", and "Lucrezia" Fantasies all underwent revision, the two last the most thorough.

There are numerous pianoforte works by the Master which are worthy of mention in addition to the accepted list. Among them those dedicated to the works of Beethoven are in the first rank, and the symphonies first of all. Alterations also occur in the second edition of this "pianoforte score". There are three editions of Beethoven's "Adelaïde" varying from one another. A "grand cadenza" is added in the second edition (it might be called a modulating improvisation) which is slightly modified in the third edition.

The more one plunges into Liszt's ideas for pianoforte transposition the more stimulating is the effect produced by the intertwining "paraphrasing thread" which persists through the numerous transformations of the same motive. I will mention just as one example Berlioz' *Symphonie Fantastique*. Liszt transcribed the whole of it for the pianoforte, then improvised on *L'Idée fixe* in an *Andante Amoroso*[1] which is used again as an introduction to the *Marche au Supplice*. Finally it was transcribed twice, in different ways and also separately—that is, independently of the Andante Amoroso or the remaining movements of the symphony.

Finally I come to the enumeration of the works hitherto omitted which have opus numbers. It is easy to understand why they should be mentioned here and not at the beginning. They belong to the most varied categories of the pianoforte works. We have classified them distinctly and all that now remains to be done is to arrange every numbered opus in proper order. By this the connection which might not have been clear at the

[1] "Nouvelle édition, augmentée d'une grande cadence par F. Liszt..." (Leipzig, Breitkopf & Härtel).

beginning, is thus clearly shown. They follow the numbers in succession:

Op. 1. *Études en douze Exercises* (*Études d'exécution transcendante*). *Travail de la Jeunesse.*

Op. 1. (Sic) *Fantaisie sur la Tyrolienne de la Fiancée.* (*Fantasie über "die Braut" von Auber*). Not satisfied with his first op. 1 Liszt decided presumably to start afresh.

Op. 2. *Fantaisie sur la Clochette de Paganini.* This, the succeeding work to the *Braut* Fantasy, probably reflects his impressions of Paganini's playing, and the simple boldness of the design, the experimental daring of the pianoforte passages, and the exuberant wealth of ingenious details is the clearest mirror of Liszt's first virtuoso period.

Op. 3. *Impromptu sur deux motifs de Spontini et de Rossini.*

Op. 4. *Deux Allegri de Bravoura.* Of which only the first *Allegro de Bravoura*, op. 4, was published by Kistner.[1] Judging from the style, op. 3 and 4 might have been composed still earlier than the *Braut* Fantasy—both can only claim the historical interest of a youthful work.

Op. 5, No. 1. *Fantaisie romantique sur deux mélodies suisses.* (*Années de Pèlerinage*).

No. 2. *Rondo fantastique sur un thème espagnol "El Contrabandista".*

No. 3. *Divertissement sur la Cavatina de Pacini: i tuoi frequenti palpiti.* (*Fantasie über die Niobe—v.* Opera fantasies).

This opus must be considered Liszt's first important creation. In its entirety it gives a concentrated picture of the Master's three characteristic ways of creation. The first piece is the model for his poetic pianoforte style as shown in the *Années* and the *Harmonies*; the second as example for the diabolical humour met with in the "Mephisto" Waltzes, the *Faust* Symphony, and in many passages of other works; the third, finally, as a type of opera paraphrase.

Op. 6. *Grande Valse de Bravoure* (*v. Valses Caprices*).

[1] Originally Probst in Leipzig.

Op. 7. *Réminiscences des Puritains.* (Opera fantasies).

Op. 8. *Deux fantaisies sur des Motifs des Soirées Musicales de Rossini.* No. 1. "La serenata e l'orgia". No. 2. "La pastorella delle alpi e li marinari". (They were published in two different editions by Schott and later separately in the series of twelve *Soirées Musicales.*)

Op. 9. *Fantaisie sur la Juive.* (*v.* Opera fantasies).

Op. 10. *Trois airs suisses.* (*v. Années de Pèlerinage* or *Album d'un Voyageur*). 1. *Ranz des Vaches: Improvvisata.* 2. *Un soir dans les montagnes: Nocturne.* 3. *Ranz des Chèvres: Allegro finale.*

Op. 11. *Réminiscences des Huguenots.* (*v.* Opera fantasies).

Op. 12. *Grand Galop Chromatique* (one of Liszt's favourite numbers for concluding a programme; there were two transcriptions and three editions).

Op. 13. *Lucia de Lammermoor* (the first of the two *Lucia* fantasies).

I must abstain from criticism in this review and indeed from any further remark. And although an enemy of repetition I consider it fitting to quote once more one of my opening sentences from this "study". Neither complete nor exhaustive, these notes will indicate only the direction which will have to be taken in compiling a collected edition.[1]

The first editions of Liszt's works contain pianistic inventions which should not be withheld from pianists. Out of print long ago, in some cases lost, they are almost forgotten by the old and are unknown to the young.

The collected edition will bring out not only all the works, but every edition of them.[2] Apart from the artistic pleasure which they open up for players and musicians, these different versions show the development and perfecting of Liszt's view of the capacities, limits and laws of his instrument and side by side they are a guide to everyone who thinks and strives after

---

[1] In the main it had a further check as is shown by the complete edition of Liszt's works still being in the process of publication.

[2] This was carried out (1922).

those heights which up to now have only once been climbed.

FOREWORD TO THE STUDIES BY LISZT*

THE Studies, the work on which Liszt was occupied from childhood to manhood should, we consider, be put at the head of his pianoforte compositions. There are three reasons for this. The first is that by giving them this position the fact is established that they are thought to be his earliest publication. Liszt's autograph catalogue (Breitkopf & Härtel, 1855) which puts the studies first of all, is the second reason. The third and strongest reason is that the studies in their entirety, give as do no other of his works, the picture of Liszt's pianistic personality in seed, in growth and finally in self-clarification.

These fifty-eight pianoforte pieces alone would place Liszt in the rank of the greatest "pianoforte" composers since Beethoven, Chopin, Schumann, Alkan, Brahms. The collected edition, of which the studies form scarcely the tenth part, will prove that Liszt towers above these composers in his command over pianistic forms.

It will give a picture of him in many lights and in many attitudes and through it we learn to know and to study the sides of his personality which differ most widely—the Mephistophelian and the Religious: he who acknowledges God does not value the Devil less—the sentimental and the inspired. Here you find the acknowledged interpreter of every style, besides the astonishing transformation artist who can wear the costume of any country with the delusive airs of a native. This collected edition will reveal a pianoforte work that draws into its circle the musical compositions of all languages, nations, and epochs from Palestrina to *Parsifal*; Liszt recreated what he took from them—a creator in a double sense.

We witness his transformation from demon to angel from the first *Fantaisie de Bravoure sur la Clochette de Paganini* (on a

* Berlin, September 1909.

diabolical suggestion of Paganini's), on to the childlike mysticism of the *Weihnachtsbaum* in which that final simplicity, the fruit of all his experience, sounds strangely from over the border of "a better land". . . .

Here he casts a magic spell and there bewitches, here his aim is to awaken feeling, there to stimulate imagination, and he is always inexhaustible in embellishments. An eye-witness relates how Liszt—pondering over a cadenza—sat down at the piano and tried three or four dozen variations of it, playing each one right through until he had made his choice.

The secret of Liszt's ornamentation is its symmetry. A classic's certainty of form is united with the freedom of improvisation, the harmony of a revolutionary lies within the calm hand of a ruler—the melodic genius of the Latin race flowers above the serious mind of the northerner. Ringing through it all and making everything golden is his sense of sound and the piano rules over all, lending wings to the course of his conception; and as Liszt's Idea gives the pianoforte its language, a mutual interplay of happy give and take is created and the boundaries of anticipation and response merge imperceptibly one into the other.

As interpreter alone Liszt shows the art of keeping the listener's attention on the stretch for points which never fail to appear, and when they appear, never disappoint.

The building and the construction in his Fantasies is inimitable. The distribution of contrasts, the admirable choice of characterising moments and motives. And here, also, the pianistically ornamental and non-essential parts of the work, used partly for characterisation and partly in the service of the instrument, are never without their purpose—they, as it were, fill the melodic branches with leaves and flowers. The way in which Liszt ennobles the trivial, enlarges the small, pushes forward what is important, and develops what is great, is all shown incontestably in the Fantasies and transcriptions. In this complete edition these take their place as one half, and not the less important one, of Liszt's genius for the pianoforte.

The main substance of this series of Studies consists in the following:

(a) Twelve *Études d'exécution transcendante*
(b) Six *Bravour-Studien nach Paganini*
(c) *Ab-irato*
(d) Three *Études de Concert*
(e) *Waldesrauschen* and *Gnomenreigen*

(a) *The Twelve Great Studies*

THERE are three editions of them and they are all collected here. The first appeared in Frankfurt in 1826. It was furnished with a picture of the young Liszt, a lithograph, which foreshortens the boyish head, and gives him romantic distorted eyes. It is difficult to determine his age from the portrait but it might have been drawn some years before the music was printed. Under it is written: "Franz Liszt, Pianist", and the title page runs:

Études
pour le Piano-Forte
en quarante-huit exercises
Dans tout les Tons Majeurs et Mineurs
Composées et dediées
à
Mademoiselle Lidie Garella
par
Le jeune Liszt
En quatre Livraisons contenant douze Études chaque
Oeuvre 6
à Paris
chez Dufaut et Dubois, Éditeurs de Musique.
Rue de Gros Chenet No. 2 et Boulevard
Poissonnière No. 10
chez Boisselot Éditeur de Musique
à MARSEILLE
Propriété de Boisselot

It is noticeable that the word *Étude* in the title is in the singular. Further, that the work was planned in forty-eight pieces, and this number should have been the first of four, but it stopped short with this single one. Finally, that it takes the opus number 6. I was able to ascertain, as a matter of fact, that there are two volumes of Variations, op. 1 and 2, which precede these early works, and an Impromptu, op. 3, and *Deux Allegri de Bravoura*, op. 4.

On the other hand there is presumably a fifth opus of which there is no record, and which cannot be found.

That Hofmeister published this self-same volume of Studies as op. 1, shows that it was the first work of Liszt's *published in Germany*.

Hofmeister's edition differs also in the title. This title page, the letters of which are executed in copper print and framed with a kind of lithographic drawing, runs thus:

Études
Pour le
Piano
En douze Exercices
composées
par
F. Liszt
Oeuvre 1
Travail de la Jeunesse
Liv. 1 16 Gr. Liv. II, 20 Gr.
Leipsig. Chez Fr. Hofmeister.

The reduction of the forty-eight exercises to twelve and the little tailpiece "youthful work" almost asking for indulgence, points to a later time of publication. I will mention at once the fact that the next printed work of Liszt's *Fantasie über die Braut von Auber* appeared in the year 1829, again with the opus number 1, and that a second (*La Clochette*) soon followed it; the numbers

3 and 4 are not repeated; instead of it the two numbers of *Apparitions* appeared in their place and the first number of *Harmonies poétiques et religieuses* (both 1834) without opus number. Then the numbering was continued from 5 to 13 (with the omission of many works occurring between) and goes on up to the year 1838.

In 1837 the new edition of the twelve studies without opus number appeared almost at the same time in Paris, Vienna and Milan.

We can now compare the first setting with the second. The Liszt whom we meet here has shot up to an unexpected height. The boy of the first setting where awakening was still in the future is not recognisable in the wonderful youth. Apparently without transition, he surpassed all available and imaginable possibilities of the piano and he never made such an immeasurable stride again. It is true that later in his search for poetic transparent sounds and by using his resources more sparingly for effects aimed at more surely he climbed still higher—into an even more refined atmosphere—and it is only in the third period that the far more inner penetrating sweetness of his maturity is harvested. Finally, he arches the bridge to childhood by employing what is seemingly most spontaneous and what is deceivingly self-evident. A turning back which is not a going back; for the man stands in a different way on the same sure place of the bank, before and after he has crossed and recrossed the stream. The primitiveness in creation and form is of two different kinds. At first he learnt how to fill out and afterwards he learnt how to leave out.

The French, Austrian and Italian impressions of the second setting correspond with each other. They are divided into two parts and in France and Austria are dedicated to Czerny. But the Ricordi edition only dedicates the first part to his teacher, the second part Liszt (or the publisher?) dedicates "à Frederic Chopin". The Haslinger impression has this title:

24
Grandes Études
Pour le Piano
composées et dediées
À Monsieur Charles Czerny
par
F. Liszt
Vienne chez Tob. Haslinger

Always *twenty-four* while both the parts only contain twelve! Nothing followed in this plan either, and there were never more than twelve studies. Both the editions came into Robert Schumann's hands at the same moment; and he wrote about them in detail in his own *Neuen Zeitschrift für Musik*, 1839 (Rob. Schumann, *Gesammelte Schriften über Musik und Musiker*, 2 Vols). "Closer inspection proves then", he writes, "that most of the pieces of the later work are only a revision of that youthful work which had already appeared many, perhaps twenty years ago in Lyons." (We have learnt that they came out eleven years previously in Marseilles.) Schumann's comparison passes sentence unfavourably on the new version "where we are often uncertain whether we do not envy the boy more than the man, who seems unable to arrive at any peace!"

A *Davidsbündler* expects—demands—from one who is twenty-six years old, and above all from the twenty-six-year-old Liszt, that he should attain to peace!

In the renunciation of his opinions as a *Davidsbündler* Schumann goes still further, since from such accusations as "lack of study", the "backwardness of the composer compared with the virtuoso", and other criticisms, he draws the conclusion that it was "indeed too late" after the salutary meeting with Chopin "for the extraordinary virtuoso to make up for what he misses as a composer". With these and still sharper words Schumann represents the twenty-six-year-old Liszt in the full maturity of his powers who "with his eminently musical

nature . . . should also have become an important composer"
as someone hopeless, and at the same time unjustly forgets to
think of his own late development.

Then Schumann proceeds to a comparison of the opening
bars of different studies out of both editions. These examples,
inscribed with "formerly" and "now", are chosen in an
amateurish way, for it is not from the opening bars that the
outward and inward growth of Liszt's gift are seen, but much
more from the completely altered plan of many of these
studies, and from the new spirit which blows through the later
ones.

These examples from the first, fifth and ninth numbers, are
right in their numbering just as, on the whole, what Schumann
says is right about the differences in the first five. But then he
commits an obvious error if (with reference to the second
edition) he is of the opinion that "the three that follow now
are 'quite new', namely the numbers 6, 7, and 8". This is only
applicable to the seventh which becomes the "Eroica" later. The
source of the sixth and eighth is present—clearly!—in the
corresponding numbers of the first version; and as he has
already cited opening bars Schumann could have proved a
connection between the introduction of the Impromptu, op. 3,
and the introduction of the seventh, a connection which exists
in reality.

But in case the reader should perchance misunderstand him,
Schumann comes back to this erroneous statement towards the
end of his report. "Numbers 6, 8 and 11 of the Hofmeister
edition are omitted in the new one (their places are taken by
these three new ones); perhaps Liszt will bring them into the
next volume for he will certainly work through the whole
circle of keys". Schumann's report ends with the following
major half close, which, to us, is more significant: "It was with
these studies that he [Liszt] made such an amazing effect during
his last visit to Vienna. But great results presume great causes,
and an audience does not allow itself to be enthusiastic over
nothing."

Between this second and the final third edition of the studies, there comes a rather different and enriched setting of the fourth study (in Paris with Maurice Schlesinger, later, with Haslinger in Vienna). In the French edition the five introductory bars added previously, are reproduced on the first page in facsimile of Liszt's handwriting. Above them for the first time is the poetic title "Mazeppa" and to the right of them is a dedication —"à Victor Hugo"—otherwise "Mazeppa" coincides in text and in general conception with the fourth study and only at the end does that kingly D major flourish surprise us, which, still an embryonic formation, here was to become a separate part in the symphonic poem of the same name. The explanatory last line of the original poem is only brought in musically; the words "il tombe enfin! . . . et se relève Roi" were first introduced in the third complete edition.

This final third and most complete edition (published in 1852 by Breitkopf & Härtel) means for us the entire Liszt, for from now on technique goes side by side with the idea as assistant to it! Would that everyone who is not yet in touch with Liszt might above all be impressed with this fundamental thought.

With the exception of the seventh study ("Eroica") which, to me, in the second setting has broader characteristics and more uniformity, all the studies find their irrevocable form here for the first time.

The final improvements in Liszt's compositions for the piano are to be found in a greater ease and smooth playableness and a corresponding amount of impressive effect and character. For instance the F minor study in the second setting presents almost insurmountable difficulties if the speed, the required fire in execution, and the correct performance of details are taken into account. Apart from this tenth and the second study they all have *poetic titles*.

The "Preludio" is less a prelude to the cycle than a prelude to test the instrument and the disposition of the performer after stepping on to the concert platform. The next piece: one of those Paganini devilries similar to those in the *Fantaisie sur la Clochette* and the *Rondo Fantastique sur un Thème Espagnol.*

"Paysage": a calm renunciation of everything worldly—taking breath during the contemplation of nature, a self-contemplation but not quite without passion; this was only achieved completely by the later Liszt.

"Mazeppa" a symphonic poem for the pianoforte which has already been discussed.

In "Feux Follets" ornament is united with colour. Their combination, which reaches its summit in *Les Jeux d'Eau à la Villa d'Este* was not without influence in the origin of Wagner's *Waldweben* and *Feuerzauber*. (The "Catholic" Liszt perhaps exercised a still more forcible influence on his great friend; which was willingly admitted by Wagner and acknowledged in *Parsifal*.)

In "Vision" we may think—so we learn from the super-scription—of the funeral of the first Napoleon, advancing with solemn and imperial pomp.

The "Eroica", more defiant than heroic, begins falteringly, then sweeps up to a climax, which has all the characteristics of Liszt's brilliance.

"Wilde Jagd" displays the strongest orchestral colouring—and there is in it, as in the *Dante* Sonata, a foundation for the symphonic poem as it was realised in César Franck's *Chasseur Maudit*.

"Ricordanza" gives the impression of a bundle of faded love letters from a somewhat old-fashioned world of sentiment.

The title "Appassionata" would well suit the following F minor Study and the whole bell-like magic of the pianoforte extends with flattering and impetuous charm over *Harmonies du Soir*.

"Chasse-neige", the noblest example, perhaps, amongst all music of a poetising nature—a sublime and steady fall of snow which gradually buries landscape and people.

(b) *The Paganini Studies*

THE first and second editions of the Paganini Studies run concurrently with the second and third of the Great Studies.

1837 Second edition of the Studies
1838 First edition of the Paganini Studies
1852 Third edition of the Studies
1851 Second edition of the Paganini Studies

Instead of being based on his childhood's work as was the case with the Great Studies, the Paganini Studies are altogether original.

The genealogy would be incomplete, however, without adding the immediate successor of the Paganini Studies, and the ancestor of the third study. I mean the *Grande Fantaisie de Bravoure sur la Clochette de Paganini* published in 1834 in Paris and (later?) by Mechette in Vienna with the opus number 2. It is composed of a free, slow introduction, a capricious fleeting anticipation of thematic material, leading up to a connecting sentence which is brought to a climax by the most daring bravura; the theme, a *Variation à la Paganini* and a *Finale de Bravura*. The care, choice and minuteness of detail given to the directions for performance in these most youthful pieces by Liszt (like *Apparitions, Harmonies poétiques, Fantaisie Romantique Suisse*, etc.) leave almost no doubt regarding the pianist-composer's intentions. The method for their execution is marked out step by step and suggestions are even made for the purely pianistic performance (as for example: "Marquez les 6 temps de la mesure en jetant la main avec souplesse"). For this reason they are worth the closest attention and are instructive for the Liszt style. The work itself, in spite of many abnormalities, is penetrated with an unusual spirit, a strangely oppressed feeling, struggling for expression. The series of Paganini Studies follows it, of which the third takes up the bell-like motive again, whilst the remaining five are taken from the

Violin Caprices. The Vienna publication of Haslinger gives them their titles in two languages:

Études
d'Exécution Transcendante
d'après Paganini
Bravour-Studien
nach
Paganini Capricen
für das Pianoforte bearbeitet
und der
Frau Clara Schumann geborenen Wieck
K. K. Kammervirtuosin
gewidmet
von
F. Liszt

As a kind of homage to Clara's husband (worldly-wise or a Mephistophelian whim?) over the first of these studies is printed Liszt's predecessor's treatment of it: "Cette seconde version est celle de Mr. Robert Schumann."

There are in existence two different versions by Liszt of the fourth study, so both volumes really contain eight altogether instead of six studies.

The manner of transcription has the true Paganini *diablerie*, "of such a kind", remarks the critic Schumann, "as may even cost Liszt some study. Whoever masters these variations (Study No. 6) as they should be mastered, in an easy, entertaining way, so that they glide past us like different scenes in a marionette show, may travel confidently all over the world and will return with golden laurels, a second Paganini-Liszt".

Clearly conscious of the hint contained in this sentence, a second transcription was made by Liszt—twelve years later—in which the obvious aim—namely "the easy entertaining manner of a marionette show" became practicable. The result of a comparison of both these editions is almost richer in disclosures than in that of the Great Studies. The way in which simplification and concentration are poured together produces "slickness" as though by a conjuring trick. Thus we see the fourth study in the second edition reduced from a previous four- and six-voice part to a one-voice part; the notes of which are restricted to one stave.

"La Campanella", the third study, has become quite unified in "one throw" here (it is difficult to believe very much in "throws"; this one lasted from the year 1834 to 1851!)

With the exception of "La Campanella" the studies bear no explanatory titles. Only to violinists the fifth is well known as "La Chasse". Without hesitation one can call the first "Il Tremolo" and the second—after the tempo prescribed—"Andante Capriccioso". The fourth, "Arpeggio", and the last "Tema e Variazioni".

(c) *Ab-irato* (d) *Trois Études de Concert* (e) *Waldesrauschen and Gnomenreigen.*

A NEW link in the chain of studies appeared in 1840 under the ceremonious and yet in no way suitable title *Morceau de Salon Étude de Perfectionnement de la Méthode des Méthodes* (an educational work published by Moscheles and Fetis).

This fruitful year saw the completion of Schubert's *Winterreise*, the publication of the *Sonnambula* Fantasy, the *Rákoczy* March, the first attempt at the Hungarian Rhapsodies (*Magyar Dallók*), and also the first transcription of the Mendelssohn and Beethoven songs, and the pianoforte score of the Beethoven Septet.

The study *Morceau de Salon*, etc., appeared revised in 1852, at a time when Liszt sorted and put in order his pianoforte compositions, gathering them together almost as if they were his last Will and Testament. In the new edition it was called *Ab-irato* and like its elder sister was published by Schlesinger in Berlin.

The three *Études de Concert* came out (1848) before this revision, and they bear throughout no revolutionary physiognomy (with the exception of the date); the Paris edition, otherwise unchanged, christened them *Caprices Poétiques* and named them successively and separately "Il lamento", "La leggierezza", "Un sospiro". Liszt's latest work of the species are the two *Études de Concert*, "Waldesrauschen" and "Gnomenreigen", composed for the Lebert and Stark (Cotta) school of pianoforte playing and incorporated in the same in 1863. They were published independently by Bahns Verlag in 1869.

In spite of taking all possible trouble I have, unfortunately, not been able to establish successfully whether or not differences exist in the publications of 1863 and 1869, as neither the firm of the Cotta edition, nor the K. Bibliothek in Berlin, nor the Liszt Museum in Weimar, nor I myself, possesses the first publications.

From the material in the six studies last discussed, one must conclude that Liszt had not exhausted himself with the very extended work on the Great Studies and the Paganini Studies, but yet had come to the end of this subject. This meant that he was relieved of an important task, while the stragglers were more like the children of mood and opportunity. Who would like to miss them? Not we who wish to preserve in this collective edition Liszt's smallest variations as he wrote them sometimes in a pupil's book. For, with a phenomenon that digresses and changes so much from the rule as that of Franz Liszt, it is often the fleeting idea seized by chance which is the characteristic one, and once vanished—it cannot be recaptured.

IX

ABOUT VARIOUS COMPOSERS

ARRIGO BOITO*

I FIND amongst my notes, in the year 1886, the following sentence: "The appearance of Boito's second opera *Nero* on which he has been working for almost twenty years, has been anxiously awaited for a long time but up till now in vain." (Graz *Tagespost*).[1] A year later I wrote in the Leipziger *Neue Zeitschrift für Musik*[2] an article which I here reproduce.

Boito, according to the Italian papers, in order to give Verdi another opportunity to express himself in music, has interrupted the composition of his opera *Nerone* and has written the libretto for *Otello*. The composition of *Nerone* underwent a further interruption through Boito writing the libretto for *Falstaff*. After sacrificing himself to assist Verdi with the latter achievement it appears that Boito occupied himself uninterruptedly with his own work for about fifty years. Now he has departed this life without having lived to see his *Nerone* on the stage, and it appears that even on his deathbed he made his intentions known about certain alterations in the score. Such a case is unique in the history of music; it may be supposed that a similar destiny has been experienced by people who have remained unknown, but then it concerned no one but themselves and it even concerned themselves with a different kind of importance. With Boito the ever-increasing responsibility of

---

* Written in June 1918.
[1] "Musikzustände in Italien", Graz *Tagespost*, 20th October 1886.
[2] "Verdi's *Otello*, A critical study", 23rd March 1887.

fulfilling his promise, which had been given publicly, became an enormous accumulation of interest in arrears. After twenty years, tendency and taste had already changed and been outstripped, especially in cases where he himself had set the fashion. In spite of this, the nation's confidence in Boito is strong; it expects *Nerone* to surpass the unsurpassable; it even demands as much and considerably more than he promised. Meanwhile famous masters arise, whose compositions are produced in rapid succession.

Boito after being in the vanguard has slowly become one who looks back, turning away from the present. At variance with himself, and continually balancing accounts with himself, he makes changes in the composition incessantly. He has matured and has passed the Boito of the first act and the craftsmanship of the beginner does not satisfy him any longer, here his juniors have got in front of him. He studies Johann Sebastian Bach, and Beethoven's last quartets. Nevertheless he wants to remain an Italian and so, not in vain, he places himself in the service of the old Verdi, for he wishes to have his share in the perfection of Italian opera. He wishes, unconsciously, to play his trumps against Richard Wagner, to hold up a great example to the young, and to allow them to feel their insignificance. He revises his work again and again and the moment for the performance approaches with increasing probability. Already once or twice, the date has been publicly fixed and advertised. The old suspense is awakened, only it is more intense, more full of demands; an entirely new generation takes it over from hearsay for they have all heard of the *Nerone* which will come one day. With sharp eyes, youth places itself in the front rank and watches. To Boito it must surely seem as if everyone were pointing a finger at him. The situation alarms him, he is determined not to cause disappointment, not to disappoint himself; if this moment fails, then a whole life fails. At the last moment the performance is countermanded—Boito takes back his score, if he has really ever allowed it out of his hand, and begins to "rewrite" it anew. But he still counts with certainty on the victory of the will. He is positive the work will be finished, only as it is now it is not yet as it should be. Every time I went to see him during the course of the last fifteen years he was "just" putting the finishing touches to the score. But now that is past, and in his biography how is one to establish what it is that was rare in this artist, on what occasion did this phenomenon first show his capacity for what was almost immense?

As a young man of five and twenty, Boito had undertaken a plan of the greatest magnitude, and carried it out so far that the execution of what he had done at least produced a work. To have the idea, at that time, and in Italy too, of setting the whole of Goethe's *Faust* to music is a fact which challenges attention. Nothing daunted, Boito, an excellent poet even when young—later he developed into an eminent connoisseur of the language—undertook the translation of Goethe's text and at the same time remodelled it in order to make it fit into what was required by the prevailing views on forms for music-drama existing at that time. Boito, in his way of construing and executing these views (which are old-fashioned and childish today) was revolutionary and unreasonable. So the public opinion was that the first performance in 1868 in Milan was a complete failure. For the young author had not only to fight against his obscurity, against tradition, and against anti-Wagnerism, but also the typical *Faust* opera by Charles Gounod which was well-established even in those days. On the way Boito's comprehensive plan had shrunk perceptibly and of Goethe's entire *Faust* really only pictures and "catch-phrases" remained, and the doubtful compromise between that which was newly desired and what was inherited from the past produced a striking and sharp effect in the first part of *Mefistofele*. Nevertheless in 1875, *Mefistofele* experienced a victorious readmission into Bologna, the town of music, and from then onwards Boito's opera found its way and was successful everywhere. "And now children, I am going to write *Nerone*", Boito may have cried to his friends, that decisive night at the theatre. And since that evening *Nerone* has existed in Italy, and become well known; as well known, unseen, and unheard as the Emperor Nero himself, but powerful and mysterious.

I got to know Boito personally when I was introduced to him by Mancinelli, in Arezzo. It was, I believe, in the year 1882 that a combined music exhibition and musical festival was held in Arezzo. This happened on the occasion of the unveiling of Aretimer's monument to Guido Monaco. *Mefistofele* was performed as the festival opera; I was engaged at the exhibition as exhibitor of the pianofortes. Boito was forty, I was sixteen; I was allowed to be present at the opera rehearsals and I learnt the opera by heart, enthusiastic about it and the composer. Boito, cultured, charming and simple, interested himself in me in the most kindly way. I owed it to him that Mancinelli, during the following winter, had one of my compositions, a big Cantata (for solo, chorus and orchestra), performed in Bologna. I shall never forget that Boito much later on was indignant with me for having devoted too much time to the pianoforte and too little time to composition. In this opinion of my artistic duty he stood almost quite alone and I absorbed this reproach as the most excellent praise and it served me as very beneficial encouragement. For this alone, if for nothing else, I should preserve a grateful and honoured remembrance of him.

REMINISCENCES OF SAINT-SAËNS *

IF one wished to speak of a Mozart school there would not be many names to mention but those few are very important. At the head of the list are those three masters of undisputed importance: Rossini, Cherubini, and Mendelssohn.

Of late years Mozart's influence has worked with less decided intensity and perhaps for this reason was even less

* Written in Berlin, December 1921, published in *Vossische Zeitung*.

vigorous in France. In style and technique he influenced the compositions of Gounod and Bizet, and finally Saint-Saëns also. The sense of pleasing sound and beauty of form is equally marked in all of these composers.

A clever person said to me once, very pertinently, that it was one of the characteristics of a Mozart score that the performance of his own part gave enjoyment to each single player. One can also observe this characteristic very much in Saint-Saëns' works, where every instrument employed is treated with equal skill and effect.

One circumstance (amongst others) which is a praiseworthy characteristic of the Mozart school is that they are clearly conscious of their limitations and wisely refuse to overstep them.

However, Saint-Saëns' limitations were not very narrow. He had already acquired fame as a brilliant pianist and organist quite early in life, and in his later compositions for the pianoforte he proved himself to be one of the few who had comprehended Liszt's pianistic mind. He had listened to the Master in his youth, with intelligent attention, and used to say that the good furtune of hearing Liszt play which had fallen to his lot, consoled him for having been born so early. From the very first his fame as pianist stood in the way of the young Saint-Saëns as composer. He shared this destiny with Liszt, but while Liszt's fame as a pianist, even now, beyond the grave, still eclipses his renown as a composer, the French Master's death today, would be announced as that of the composer Saint-Saëns.

History has not yet recorded the case of a composer of established renown developing, subsequently, into a great pianist; whilst the case of a composer's fame triumphing later and putting his earlier fame as a pianist in the shade can be considered the rule, with few exceptions. It can be read of Johann Sebastian Bach in Hawkins' *History of Music* written in the eighteenth century "that he was an organist of renown who had also composed some excellent pieces of music"! Among well-known composers in history who first made a sensation as pianists I will mention, for example, Mozart, Beethoven, Mendelssohn, Meyerbeer, Weber and Chopin. Bruckner, above all, was an astonishing organist, Brahms to begin with toured as a pianist, and Liszt's case is better known than rightly appreciated. Amongst the names of great composers who stepped at once on to the field as composers I can only mention, Wagner, Berlioz and Verdi. Strengthened by this consciousness of these last examples, a group of composers, in part rightly appreciated, arose during the last twenty-five years who could only give an indication of their own compositions on the keyboard with one finger. The logical development of this generation is that it has again brought forth a group of composers who do not trouble themselves at all as to whether, or in what way, their creations can be performed. If we look back from this present state (which is certainly transitory) to Saint-Saëns' personality, we see in him a figure that is rounded-off on every side.

To achieve such a well-proportioned rounding-off, natural gift, industry, intelligence and favourable circumstances are necessary. Natural gifts did not fail Saint-Saëns in any way. I was often told in Paris how he would write a new composition directly into the score and at the same time keep up a quick-witted conversation with friends and guests. Moreover, the score would turn out to be calligraphically clean, and ready for printing. He seemed to indulge in composition as a pleasant mental exercise; he was a cheerful priest of the art. One cannot gather from his music whether he was good, kind or capable of suffering.

In any case his disposition apparently was armed against exhausting emotions; he was not in the least sentimental. I remember an evening in Brussels, in which we (his publisher Durand, Ysaÿe and I) accompanied him from the hotel to the theatre where the fiftieth performance of his *Samson and Delilah* was to be given as a gala performance. We were all in rather a festive mood but Saint-Saëns seemed thoughtful too. Half way

there he stopped and begged us to excuse him for a moment—
when he last passed through Brussels he had left an old hat to
be done up which he wished to fetch before the hatter shut
his shop.

It is true that from his seventieth year onwards, he turned
away from Wagner, an attitude which he held consistently
and boldly. This was taken so amiss in Paris where, since the
last decade, it is good form to be a lover of Wagner, that at a
party when he was eighty-three people who were present
turned their backs on him because on the previous day he had
expressed his opinion about Wagner in public.

A respected musical paper snatched this opportunity to
insult "the well-known composer of the Wedding Cake".
Youth disowned him completely and he complained bitterly
(but without pathos) that he only passed for "scrap iron".

There was nothing in him either daemonic or "devout".
He did not soar above the earth but he stood on it as Grand
Seigneur, a nobleman in the realm of music.

RICHARD STRAUSS*

AMONG the living German composers who have become
well known he is the most conspicuous. He is to Wagner and
Liszt as the Baroque is to the Renaissance, as Veronese to
Titian, and Tiepolo to Veronese. He is "slimmer" and less
heavy than Wagner, more stormy, more complicated than
Liszt because he is smaller. He can only give what is small in
small forms, the bigness of the form stands there for the bigness
of the idea.

He views the whole human world as a musical subject. He
gets stranded in the supernatural, because he pulls it down to
human level.

His ideas of love, heroes, passion, grief, are conventional

* Unpublished typed copy among the written posthumous works, without
date or signature. Preserved in the German State Library in Berlin.

without arriving at the dimensions of the popular. He never conquers certain deficiencies. Excellent orchestrator as in fact he is, he comes to grief over sound-combinations that don't sound. Master of form as he is, he yet falls anew into dilemmas.

Salome*

... That in its harmonic and orchestral part it shows a score commanding the highest respect.

That the libretto is a theatrical poem of gifted ingenuity, and the natural final fruit of a long genealogy: the Bible—plastic art of the Renaissance—Gustave Flaubert.

In art everything changes step by step. With this *Salome* such a step may have been taken on the top of other manifestations which will hurry on to the ascent of a new and higher step. Every son has the stuff of his ancestors in him— by his side flourish a hundred other species.

Sinfonia Domestica†

I HAVE the score of R. Strauss' *Sinfonia Domestica* with me on board. Strauss is a person of decided talent and has rich gifts. Polyphony and movement are necessary elements in him.

In this piece, the musical illustration misses fire (I have only read it) for the child's cry is the only thing not to be misunderstood, provided one knows the title beforehand. It is a long work consisting of small movements, and the movements of small motives. He uses much material from his earlier compositions. Like a family picture, it is very joyless, irritable, excited and restless. The score looks like the streets in New York. Its name is the only effective thing about the oboe d'amore, that old instrument, the deeper oboe, but who hears the name when it is played? The frequent use of a complete clarinet family, as in chamber music, must make a pretty colour effect (a family within a family).

* Opinions about *Salome* from *Die Zeit*, May 1907.
† Letter to his wife, 27th March 1904.

A masterly fugue.

A scherzo, a cradle song, both according to recipe, without surprises. A couple of well-known climaxes which come from *Tristan*. It breaks off frequently and begins again. Contains lyrical and popular trivialities (the latter by polka rhythms, as used previously in *Till Eulenspiegel* in *Don Quixote* and *Feuersnot*). An admirable facility for making things complicated and spreading out what is small. Strauss seems to write out both the principal voices, then the principal middle voice, and afterwards cram in everything there is still room for in between. One can go on and on with that, and he does not stop in time. He does not understand the *mastery of the unfinished*. On the whole, a work for which one has the greatest respect, from which one gets much amusement, and in which there are many quotations (especially technical ones). This is as far as the first impression goes.

Yesterday evening I turned over the leaves of Richard Strauss' score again.* It gains nothing from renewed acquaintance.

His orchestration—in spite of unusual virtuosity—is not "sonorous" because his style of composing is opposed to his orchestral writing. It branches out too much. I believe he has made a mistake in some of the proportions again. He has said himself: "Wagner makes everything sound but I am often unable to achieve this." That is because Wagner concentrates everything on the principal idea. Strauss really has twelve subordinate ideas and they are in confusion; the chief idea lies more in the atmosphere than in the motive, but is easily effaced by overloading.

But I must *hear* the work. Music is there to be heard.

Don Quixote†

I SAT in the orchestra yesterday and heard *Don Quixote* by Richard Strauss. It is a work which has great qualities;

* Letter to his wife, 2nd April 1904.
† Letter to his wife, 18th February 1911.

175

commonplace in the lyrical places, unusually exciting in the grotesque parts, naïve in a boorish way and yet on the other hand too cultivated, badly put together as regards form, but the daring texture of sound is excellent. On the whole, one of the most interesting works of our time and the richest in invention; perhaps the composer's best work.

Up to the present Toscanini is the most intelligent musician I have met (with perhaps the exception of Strauss).*

SCHÖNBERG MATINÉE†

IS sentimentality experiencing a new birth? After hearing (playing through and studying with others) Arnold Schönberg's pianoforte pieces and songs it looks almost as if it were so. Repressed tears, wafting of sighs, gusts of wind through trees of sorrow, rustling autumn leaves—here and there a brief defiance or the reflection from an early spring sun disappearing quickly. And in between some tomfoolery. Solitary voices gliding about in a recitative-ish way in unexpected intervals. It is difficult to feel in what way they belong to one another. A daring harmony, the point of which is blunted by its continuous use, short trailing phrases, taking breath frequently and listening backwards, simplicity in an almost barbarous degree. And, on the other hand, containing so much un-affectedness, clear sight, and honesty.

Finally, three pieces on two pianos for eight hands.

At the keyboards sit four young men with fine, characteristic heads: to see them place their young intelligences, submissive and efficient, at the service of what is still an unsolved riddle, makes an almost impressive effect.

At the back of the little platform glimmer two restless eyes;

* Letter to his wife, 28th February 1911.
† Written in Berlin, 1911, for *Pan*.

176

a baton waves with short, nervous movements—one can only see Schönberg's head and hand, which influence the four valiant performers by suggestion and impart his fever to them more and more.

An unusual picture which, strengthened by the unusual sound, exercises a fascination.

In any case, different from that of a sonata recital given by two court professors.

DIE BEKEHRTE *

WALDIMIR (RUDOLFOWITSCH) VOGEL is twenty-five years old, of Russian origin and a student in the Staats-akademischen composition class. Besides a feeling, arising from parentage, of rebellion against existent and accepted things, there dwells in him a vibrating soul and an individual sensibility. When the whole class received as a composition task *Die Bekehrte* by Goethe, Vogel's exposition of it, if not the most masterly, proved to be the most unusual work. In any case as the most suitable of all to figure here as a characteristic example of the "new road" in music.

The roads which pass as "new" today are new no longer. The epoch of experiments, and the over-estimation of the means of expression to the disadvantage of content and artistic durability is drawing rapidly towards its close. Enriched through it the "positive"—as opposed to what is "oppositional"—will very soon attain to its lawful rights (in order to give way once more to coming oppositions which fulfil the aim of rejuvenating it.) In this way our example also represents something distinctive rather than conclusive.

* Written in Berlin, November 1921 for *Faust*, No. 2, which bore the title "Der Kampf um den neuen Stil".

X

VARIOUS ESSAYS AND THOUGHTS

OPEN REPLY*

Very Honoured Sir and Friend,

Before I read your criticism of my first Liszt recital I had meanwhile made a note of the following opinions as an appendix, in addition to others, for a new edition of my *Aesthetic*. They are in a certain measure the answer to your criticism.

Feeling is a moral point of honour, as honesty is, a quality no one will be denied and which belongs to the currency both of life and of art. But whilst in life want of feeling may be forgiven in favour of a more splendid quality—as, for example, bravery and impartial justice—in art it is regarded as the highest moral quality.

But in music feeling requires two companions—taste and style. Now in life one finds taste as rarely as deep warm feeling and as for style it belongs to the domain of art. What is left over is an appearance of feeling which has to be expressed with tearfulness and turgidity. And before everything it must be made obvious! It must be underlined so that no one can miss seeing and hearing it. It must be thrown, greatly magnified, on the screen in the sight of the public, so that it dances obtrusively and indistinctly before their eyes.

For in life, too, expressions of feeling are shown more frequently in looks and words: rarer and more genuine is that feeling which acts without speaking and most valuable of all is the feeling which hides itself.

What is commonly understood by "feeling" is: *tenderness, pathos and extravagance of expression.*

Yet how much more there is still to be included in the wonder-

* Compare *Entwurf einer neuen Aesthetik der Tonkunst* (Insel Verlag).

flower of feeling! Restraint, forbearance, sacrifice, strength, activity, patience, generosity, joyousness and that all-controlling intelligence from which, properly speaking, feeling springs.

It is the same in art, which reflects the feelings of life, and it is still more pronounced in music which repeats the feelings of life to which, as I have emphasised, taste must be added and style—style which distinguishes Art from Life.

What the amateur or mediocre artist is concerned about is only feeling on a small scale, in detail, for short stretches.

Feeling on a large scale is mistaken by the amateur, the semi-artist, and the public (and unfortunately the critic also) for want of feeling; because they have not the power to hear large stretches as parts of a still larger whole. Therefore feeling is also economy.

Accordingly, I discern three aspects in feeling: feeling as taste, as style and as economy. Each a whole and each the third of a whole. In them and over them rules a subjective trinity. Temperament, intelligence and the sense of equipoise.

These six carry on a round dance of such subtlety in the arrangement of the coupling and intertwining of figures, of supporting and being supported, of advancing and curtseying, of movement and repose, that a dance more full of art is inconceivable.

It is wrong to dissipate feeling on what is unimportant.

As regards my interpretation of the spirit of Liszt, it is natural that this should be merged with my own individuality, as far as I possess one. But I have experienced the happiness of knowing that my instinct has rightly divined the Master's aims, because important pupils of Liszt (and among them both those whom you name) have recognised this gladly and often been moved by it. Your opinion is too valuable for me to let it pass in silence, therefore it seemed appropriate to address this reply to you as a proof of my regard.

Yours,

F. B.

ART AND TECHNIQUE*

IT is the distinguishing characteristic of the artist—I mean of the artist, and not those who merely practise an art—that he sets himself new problems continually and looks for his satisfaction in the solution of them. The dilettante, on the other hand, naturally takes advantage of every external alleviation of difficulties, whilst the artist turns from them as from a task which has been accomplished.

In this I believe I can see what the dilettante and the artist have in common and in what way they differ. Both are busy with difficulties but the dilettante hammers at those which the artist has already overcome and the artist constantly creates and conquers new ones for himself.

To those artists who strive after other perfections, the alleviation of purely technical difficulties can be helpful in furtherance of these efforts.

If it is true that "the power of expression is increased when a singer has to take trouble to sing a high note", how does the matter stand in the case where the greatest difficulties are to be found in artistically subordinate places? These will then be brought into undue prominence in consequence of the effort.

The more means the artist has at his disposal the more use will be found for them.

Art, especially music, demands freedom of movement. Up to now it has been obliged to devote most of its strength to overcoming material hindrances. What is apparently the greatest technical simplification is only equal to a man's stride in immense space.

* Reply to Dr. L. Schmidt's article on Clutsam's "Curved Keyboard" in No. 35 of *Signale*, August 1909. Also appeared in this number of *Signale*.

We commend the makers of the strides and the liberators however slight their power may be.

For where is the apparatus that man could invent and set in motion which would allow harmony's million tongues to sound? Where is and where will ever be the technique which will allow the thousand registers of the world-organ to play?

And here stands an "inquirer" in front of a pianoforte keyboard whose line diverges slightly from what is customary and fears that art will be ruined by it.

What a fragile art he must have in mind!

Have thunderstorms vanished from the world because Franklin discovered the lightning conductor?

In art, to me, every simplification of difficulty seems to mean that a new difficulty takes the place of the one already surmounted. If we agreed with the "inquirer" that "the lack of mechanical resistance makes playing more uninteresting" we only find the artist placed before a new difficulty. But of what interest it can be to the inquirer whilst listening, to see a player continually battling to overcome these resistances is unfathomable. And still more, in what way this struggle can contribute towards the preservation and salvation of art.

HOW LONG WILL IT GO ON?*

YESTERDAY we anchored off the magical south coast of Ireland. The contemplation of beauty amply made up for the loss of time. The howling of the practical aim, which groans through the world of culture, sounded farther away and that other noise, criticism, was silent. There was pureness and quietness in the air, something like a Sunday, apart from calendar and

* Written on the voyage to America, 23rd December 1910, for the magazine *Signale für die Musikalische Welt*, Berlin.

church service, which otherwise is met with only in the extreme north or in the tropics.

If, on a quiet morning, at home, I open a beloved score—the Finale of Act II from Mozart's *Figaro* for example—and spin myself into its silken web which is almost without weight, I pass into this festival atmosphere and the consciousness of heaviness ceases to exist.

Music is the most mysterious of the arts. Around it should float something solemn and festival-like. The entrance to it should be through ceremony and mystery as to a Freemasons' Lodge. It is artistically indecent that anyone from the street, railway train, or restaurant, is free to clatter in during the second movement of a Ninth Symphony.

That is why I love *The Magic Flute*, because it unites enigma with drama.

The entrance to a concert hall should give promise of something unusual and should lead us gradually from secular life to the life that is innermost. Step by step the visitor should be conducted into what is exceptional.

In order to achieve this and before everything else, the number of musical performances should be cut down. Then every one of them would rise in value, be chosen and prepared more carefully, be anticipated differently, and enjoyed differently.

Gifted beginners should not be harassed, obliged to sacrifice money and then lose what remains of their hardly-maintained courage by playing to an empty hall, but they should give their fresh and promising gifts to the world before a chosen few; a spring festival of the art, a greeting to a bud just coming into bloom, the initiation of a youthful talent, a calm and cheerful ceremony. Established performers should seldom be heard, and then only if they have something important and new to impart.

The opening of the opera should be the event of the year. The first performance of an opera should fill the public with that thrill of anticipation which is experienced before the rise of the first curtain which I, and many with me, have known from childhood upwards. And the audience should be silent, silent and concentrated, and not applaud, and nothing should be written about it for days after. How much is destroyed by clapping and criticism, how little is added! How much longer will some printed stereotyped phrases lead us round in a circle such as we read the next day that "technical dexterity is opposed to feeling—virtuosity opposed to inner comprehension"? Was not Bach a virtuoso of counterpoint, Wagner a virtuoso of the orchestra, Mozart a virtuoso of all the virtuosities? How much longer shall we be told that "Dissonance is opposed to consonance", "Transcription is opposed to composition", "Lightness is in opposition to profundity", that "An innovator is refused the inventive faculty" ("innovator" includes "inventor"), that new works are found to be too long, whereas the length of classical works is put up with and admired? A joke of Beethoven's is taken seriously and the work of someone who is not celebrated is smiled at? Or that the imitator is justly reproached but at the same time a model is held up before the eyes of one who possesses originality?

How much longer must it be before we learn that not everything old is good and not everything new is bad, and that as yet but little of the road has been travelled.

Therefore do not look backwards and do not stop still, for time knows no delay and life is limited and uncertain.

And do we not drag too much ballast on our back which hinders swift and easy going? Just what is absolutely necessary and important is cumbersome enough.

The social game of lion-hunting, too, must be stopped. Pettiness would then disappear of its own accord. How many know who was the builder of an admired cathedral? To whom does it occur to ask about him?

Finally, should not music cease to be a trivial decoration for trivial occasions like, for example, a dispenser of entertainment in restaurants and inns?

Or could not a line be drawn between the airs which may be played in such places and those from the Temple to which they alone belong? Was not Belshazzar punished because he misused the vessel from the holy of holies at his own feast?

If the art should become absolutely accessible to all (which I personally am against) let us at least preserve a distance. Let it be in the middle of the people and yet separated from them, as becomes a monarch.

And above all it must be separated from aims of gain. A way must be found to free it from this if the next century is not to shine in history as the century without art. Utopian? No! Really practical considerations, and an endeavour to move towards a *rinascimento* which in order that its progress may correspond to the boasted progress of mankind must shine more brightly than its forerunner: as the morning on the south coast of Ireland, pure and Sunday-like.

Now the whistle sounds. We swim in fog—the horn has just uttered its warning cry. . . .

ROUTINE*

ROUTINE is very much esteemed and frequently required. In musical "officialdom" it is the foremost stipulation.

Just the plain fact that routine is brought into connection with the conceptions of music at all, that it actually exists and moreover passes for a valuable attribute, shows what the views are with regard to musical art and how tightly drawn its boundaries have become and how we alienate ourselves from it.

For routine is nothing but the inclination towards some tricks of craftsmanship and their indiscriminate application to every case that presents itself.

Therefore in music there must be an astonishing number of analogous cases!

But I think in this way about music: that every case should

* Written in Berlin, August 1911, for the magazine *Pan*.

be a new case, an "exception". That every problem, once solved, should experience no repeated attempts at solution. A theatre of surprises and sudden ideas and of what is apparently unprepared; where everything is breathed out of the depth of human nature and given back to the great Cosmos, out of which it rises to man.

How helplessly the army of "routineers" would stand in front of this gentle but unsubdued force! It would be driven to flight and—disappear.

Routine transforms the Temple into a factory.

It destroys all creativeness. For creation means bringing form out of the Void.

But routine is the factory for mass production. It is "poetry made to order". It prevails because it suits the generality. It flourishes in the theatre, in the orchestra, with virtuosi and in the "Schools of Art", that is to say those institutions which are arranged excellently for the maintenance of the teachers. One is tempted to cry out "Avoid Routine!". Let every beginning be as if none had been before! Know nothing but rather think and feel and learn through being able to do!

"It is my misfortune that I possess no routine", Wagner once wrote to Liszt when the *Tristan* score was not progressing.

In this Wagner deceived himself, and before other people used the deception as a mask of defence. Obviously, he already possessed a respectable measure of routine, and his composing machinery stopped if the kind of obstacle arose which can only be overcome with the help of inspiration.

If Wagner had never possessed routine he would have made the confession without any bitterness.

Fundamentally, his subtle statement really expresses the artist's contempt for everything routine-ish. By it Wagner disowns a quality which he himself esteems but little and provides against others being able to impute it to him. He utters self-praise with an air of ironical despair. He is, in truth, unhappy that his work is at a standstill but feels himself

185

abundantly comforted by the consciousness that his gift stands above the cheap expedient of routine, and with an air of modesty he owns regretfully that the skill of craftsmanship is entirely missing in him.

The sentence is a masterpiece of self-justification and out of it sounds the warning for us: Avoid Routine!

INTRODUCTION TO E. T. A. HOFFMANN'S
*PHANTASTISCHE GESCHICHTEN**

NOTHING is more dangerous for the understanding of the artistic vision than the "slogan". It sounds arresting, it saves breath and thought, and cuts off any discussion.

The true value of the poet Hoffmann has suffered fundamentally and for a long time from the unhappily inspired and summary slogan of "The ghost-like Hoffmann". He has been classified and characterised by it. As opposed to all models for stories, ghost stories belong to a class of literature that intentionally rejects what is true. With a more intimate inspection of the deep twilights of romantic poetry it will be perceived, however, that Hoffmann seldom "invents", but rather reports what he has seen or read.

When I had the opportunity of comparing the content of *Signor Formica* with a much older biography of Salvator Rosa (a projected opera text on the same subject was the occasion for doing so) I was astonished to find confirmation of this fact; for Hoffmann, in his tale, had followed the course of the biography step for step with pedantic fidelity. But something miraculous takes place here. For how Hoffmann understands how to diffuse a glamour, a twilight of the unusual and unreal, indeterminate and indeterminable, over experiences which are often borrowed word for word, and the way in which he raises the farcical figure to the grotesque, the unique, and illuminates

* Paris, 2nd February 1914 (Georg Müller Verlag, Munich).

it with an indefinable ray of uncanniness—that is his visionary power, the gift of his unique, oscillating spirit. This element first begins to vibrate where a normal brain considered observation closed, and the ensuing result of this laying on of colour is only comparable to that something which makes things in the night appear otherwise than as we know them. It is indeed seldom that Hoffmann forsakes the reality of life, and if we get the impression of improbability, and of anything irregular and supernatural from his descriptions it will scarcely be possible to establish the moment at which this impression is born in us. Ghosts and sorcery are never represented explicitly as real happenings; over these Hoffmann leaves the reader in uncertainty. An intercepted word, overheard behind walls, gives cause for boundless forebodings without proving anything. The most unbelievable and hair-raising histories of a person are constructed from third-hand rumours, and are presented by Hoffmann in the most correct form. But generally it leaks out afterwards that the apparitions and events like conjuring-tricks were seen by a visionary, a drunkard, or someone fever-stricken or insane who saw, or thought he saw, them as reported. And the next morning, in broad daylight, everything stands in its usual place, homely and commonplace, completely divested of everything fantastic and sublime.

With no word does Hoffmann vouch for the reality of these incredible happenings; the drawing of the boundary line between what is actual and what is visionary he always leaves to the judgment of the reader. In this way again, with inimitable dexterity, he certainly reduces his listener to a condition of doubt, and yields to this doubt himself.

On the other hand, there is much that is symbolic and metaphysical in his writing which flies and flashes through the ordinary occurrences and makes a real picture with tangible figures and action, like a lizard darting through the moss. As for example, the principles of good and evil which are constantly reappearing under different aspects with Hoffmann.

Finally, reality breaks through everywhere in Hoffmann's Tales where, appearing subjectively as art enthusiast and art connoisseur, he gives expression to his amiable and grim, selectively cultured and always independent mind. This is exemplified most fully in those conversations which the *Serapionsbrüder* carry on with one another in which Hoffmann dissects himself, as it were, through five different figures, thus personifying simultaneously the many-sidedness and contradictions of his nature. These conversations are comparable to a chest full of costly and amusing bric-à-brac amongst which some pieces of outstanding value emerge (this makes me think of an essay on old and new church music which gives the impression of dying away wondrously in an unearthly distance and height at the end . . .) and they contain important comments on Hoffmann's own nature. The interpretation of his fantasy, as it has been sought here, is formulated, concisely and convincingly, in the following sentences which come from Theodore's mouth: "I think that the base of the Jacob's ladder on which a man ascends into higher regions, should be fastened into life, so that everyone can climb up after. Then if a man finds that he has climbed higher and higher into a fantastic and enchanted realm, he will believe that this realm still belongs to his life and is really the most wonderful and glorious part of it. For him it is the beautiful and splendid flower-garden outside the gate, in which he can wander at pleasure to his great delight, once he has resolved to forsake the dusty walks of the town."

THE REALM OF MUSIC:

AN EPILOGUE TO THE NEW AESTHETIC*

COME, follow me into the realm of music. Here is the iron fence which separates the earthly from the eternal. Have you

* Letter to his wife, 3rd March 1910.

undone the fetters and thrown them away? Now come. It is not as it was before when we stepped into a strange country; we soon learnt to know everything there and nothing surprised us any longer. Here there is no end to the astonishment, and yet from the beginning we feel it is homelike.

You still hear nothing, because everything *sounds*. Now already you begin to differentiate. Listen, every star has its rhythm and every world its measure. And on each of the stars and each of the worlds, the heart of every separate living being is beating in its own individual way. And all the beats agree and are separate and yet are a whole.

Your inner ear becomes sharper. Do you hear the depths and the heights? They are as immeasurable as space and endless as numbers.

Unthought-of scales extend like bands from one world to another, *stationary* and yet *eternally in motion*. Every tone is the centre of immeasurable circles. And now *sound* is revealed to you!

Innumerable are its voices; compared with them the murmuring of the harp is a din; the blare of a thousand trombones a chirrup. All, all melodies heard before or never heard, resound completely and simultaneously, carry you, hang over you, or skim lightly past you—of love and passion, of spring and of winter, of melancholy and of hilarity, they are themselves the souls of millions of beings in millions of epochs. If you focus your attention on one of them you perceive how it is connected with all the others, how it is combined with all the rhythms, coloured by all kinds of sounds, accompanied by all harmonies, down to unfathomable depths and up to the vaulted roof of heaven.

Now you realise how planets and hearts are one, that nowhere can there be an end or an obstacle, that infinity lives in the spirit of all beings; that each being is illimitably great and illimitably small: the greatest expansion is like a point; and that light, sound, movement and power are identical, and each separate and all united, they are life.

A FAIRY-LIKE INVENTION*

New York, 1st April 1911
Wireless Despatch

[That we today, on 29th March, already know publicly what is only appointed to leave New York as a wireless despatch on 1st April will seem less mysterious to the reader after he has finished reading this despatch. Compared with the discovery revealed here, this tiny anticipation of it seems a mere bagatelle.—Ed.]

AN extraordinary discovery is announced from South Park-hill. Kennelton Humphrey Happenziegh, the scientist domiciled there—who is highly esteemed in professional circles but in no way celebrated   has succeeded, thanks to an unusual gift of sharp deduction, in arriving at far-reaching conclusions, through comparatively simple experiments.

K. H. Happenziegh has devoted the greatest part of his studies to the experimental criticism of acoustic phenomena, and it was well known that in a life's work he had recorded valuable observations that until now had not been made public but which were waited for with suspense in learned circles.

The nature and object of these observations he had kept strictly secret and so it had also remained a secret that, of late, Happenziegh has been occupied with the preparation of a super-sensitive apparatus (intended for phonographic disks). The contrivance, which he has perfected at last, resembles at a first glance a drum disk with a super-sensitive epidermis, and possesses the quality of combining the utmost delicacy with the most complete power of resistance and is able to pick up noises which are inaudible or unintelligible to the human ear; moreover it has the power of dissecting complicated sounds into their constituent parts. If, for example, one plays a note on the violin, every accompanying noise is picked up separate-

* Busoni's witty April joke appeared in 1911 in the magazine *Signale für die Musikalische Welt*.

ly; the sounds which arise from the hairs of the violin-bow; the resin, the pressure of the fingers which hold the bow, the most imperceptible vibration of a window pane are recorded on the disk. The contrivance is so extremely delicate that when a hand is passed through hair the crackling is *distinctly* audible; light steps in the next room are recorded by it, the slightest breath is impressed on it.

Happenziegh had arrived so far with his results when the most astonishing surprise fell to his lot through his invention.

And from here on it might be necessary to believe in the supernatural or to suppose trickery, if Happenziegh's reputation did not warrant him to be a conscientious, truthful and learned man, and if his clear calculations (which he does not withhold) did not point to the veracity of the incredible information which we shall endeavour to communicate as comprehensibly as possible.

Happenziegh left his laboratory at two o'clock in the morning, after he had completed a new and (as he believed) perfect disk, and entered it again at six o'clock after a short night's rest.

He subjected his disk to an examination by means of a very powerful microscope constructed by him for this purpose, and discovered on it certain impressions which he could not account for. After he had separated the customary noises of the town at night, which he considered as secondary phenomena in this case, he found an accumulation of obscure diagrams which were systematic, complicated, and at first unintelligible. On first consideration they might have been of musical origin although they only showed a remote relationship with the musical forms familiar to him. In any case they must have come from a very great distance.

An investigation as to whether within a ten-mile radius music might have been played that night and during those four hours, resulted in a negative answer. All restaurants were closed at this time and no private soirées had taken place. More precise information proved that there was no misunderstood genius living in this circuit and that no such person had been anywhere as guest that night. . . .

But the marks were imprinted and the disk, when it was brought into rotation, sounded music without doubt, which to the scholar's ears, however, remained as unintelligible as the diagrams had been to his eyes.

This happened about six months ago.

In between, Happenziegh had been at the work incessantly and his never-resting mind had succeeded in giving the solution to the riddle and in bringing forward a new theory which fills us with awe and astonishment and opens up the widest prospects.

As the air needs an instrument to make its vibrations perceptible to our ear, so the air itself is only an instrument which transmits the not yet fully fathomed wave-lengths. These original wave-lengths, as Happenziegh recognises, have the characteristic quality of being similarly effective in a time-sphere, as, for instance, wireless telegraphy in that of space.

In time its effect works as well backwards as forwards and its intensity decreases correspondingly with the distance.

Sound atmospherics, put in vibration through exterior impulse, continue in both directions. Its impressions will be passed on, into the past as well as into the future.

A scream fades away into tomorrow and the day after tomorrow and further, in corresponding strength—logically into yesterday and the day before yesterday also.

Thus, through a chance not yet cleared up, a demonstration of music in the future seems to have found its way on to the super-sensitive disk and to have impressed itself there.

After laborious calculations (for which quite new estimations will have to be found) the origin of the phonographic marks might lie twenty to three hundred years in front of us (according to Happenziegh's assumption). If one takes an average figure, a hundred and forty years is the result, so that music written on the disk lies about a century and a half in the future.

K. H. Happenziegh is not a musician by profession and the reports about the musical nature of his remarkable impressions sound uncertain.

The reproduction itself is very weakened and appears still more indistinct because of its strangeness. One might almost suppose that all the instruments, which one knows of or can guess at, play *muted* and that in addition to this the space in which they are placed is sharply separated from the listener.

But there are also sounds in the phenomenon whose nature is quite unknown to us and which certainly point to new sound mediums. Sounds from the trombones like Aeolean harps melt into a sound fog, and again other voices out of the void, without audible beginning, disappear into the atmosphere of sound. Sounds as if coming from tinkling water and burning fire assume melodic form, appear and disappear.

Intervals are apparently purer and show the aliveness of human breath in their gradations and combinations.

Nature itself seems to sound and we are tempted to suppose that this music never wearies and goes on creating from what is there into infinity.

All further details and additions to this sensational discovery we will communicate to our readers punctually and conscientiously every year.

Aprilus Fischer

THE ESSENCE OF MUSIC: A PAVING OF THE WAY TO AN UNDERSTANDING OF THE EVERLASTING CALENDAR*

IN the pursuance of my observations I have been gradually forced to the opinion that our conception of the essence of music is still fragmentary and dim; that only very few are able to perceive it and fewer still to grasp it, and they are quite unable to define it. My earlier realisation of the Oneness

* Written 8th June 1924. First published in the periodical *Melos*, Vol. I, 1924.

of music might pass as a premonition of what I set myself to formulate here: a premonition hitherto perceived intuitively by philosophers rather than by real musicians, because the vision of such master-minds is less impeded by considerations of technique such as preoccupy musicians. A mind of such culture came to my assistance in my endeavour to find exactitude of expression for my thoughts. The following passage, quoted from a novel by Anatole France,[1] could be taken as a motto for my own book (*Entwurf einer neuen Aesthetik der Tonkunst*, 1906): "For the content of a piece of music existed and exists complete and unalterable before and after it has sounded."

In this novel by the French master a doctor says to a young dramatist who with beating heart waits for the end of the première of his play:

"Do you not believe that everything that is to happen has already and for all time happened?"

And without waiting for an answer he adds:

"If the phenomena of the world come to our ken one after another, we must not conclude that in reality they follow one another in succession and we have still less ground for supposing that they take place at the exact moment at which we perceive them. The universe appears to us continuously incomplete and we have the illusion that it is continuously completing itself. So, as we become aware of the phenomena successively, we believe that they do in fact come into effect successively. We have the idea that those we no longer see are in the past and those we do not yet see are in the future. Yet imagine that there might be beings formed in such a way that they can see simultaneously what, for us, are past and future. One might also conceive beings who perceive the phenomena in inverse order and see them roll back from our future to our past. If, for example, we imagined such beings who could

[1] (*Histoire Comique*. Translator's note.)

194

dispose of space differently from us, and were able to move with a speed surpassing that of light, the conception these beings would have of the succession of phenomena would be very different from ours. On a clear night even *we* see what was and what is, if we turn our eyes to the ear of the Virgo, sparkling over the top of a poplar. And with an equal right we can suppose that we see what is and will be. For if the star, as it appears to us, represents the past in relationship to the tree, the tree is the future in relationship to the constellation. Yet the constellation, which shows its fiery face from afar—not as it is today, but as it was in our youth, perhaps even before our birth—and the poplar, whose young leaves tremble in the cool of the evening, appear to us at the same moment and, for us, that moment represents the present. We say a thing is in the present if we see it precisely. If we are only aware of a more indistinct picture of it we say it is in the past. A thing which might have been played out a million years ago will be the present for us as soon as we receive the sharpest possible impression of it; then it will not be in the past for us, but rather something in the present. The order in which things revolve in the depths of the Universe is unknown to us. We only know the order of our perception of them. To believe that the future does not exist because we do not know it, is the same as believing that a book is unfinished because we have not read it to the end. Through immutable destiny the Universe is constructed like a triangle of which one side and two angles are given. Things of the future are pre-ordained. From the moment this happens they are as complete as if they existed. In fact they do exist. They exist so really that in part we already know them. And if, in relationship to their endlessness this part is minute, it stands, nevertheless, in a very substantial relationship to the part of completed facts which we are able to grasp. We can go so far as to suppose that the future, for us, is not much darker than the past. We know that generation after generation will follow in work, happiness, and suffering. I strain my sight beyond the durability of the human race. I see the constellations gradually changing their forms which seemed unalterable; we know that tomorrow, and for a long time to come, the sun will rise every morning. We see the new moon of the next month. We do not see it so clearly as tonight's new moon, because we do not know in which grey or glowing sky she will show us her old saucepan of a hinder-part. But if we knew that exactly, each rising of the moon would be equally clear to us. The knowledge of certain facts is the only reason which brings us to believe in their reality. As we know of certain coming things we believe them to be real. And if they truly are real they have also become realised already. So it is believable, my dear fellow, that your play has been acted already, it may be a thousand years ago, or it may be half an hour ago—it makes no difference. If you think of that you will feel calmer."

It was while translating this fragment that it first came to my mind that I had set down something akin to it at some previous time; for, miserable human beings that we are, with similar efforts we come to the same conclusions. Inconclusive and uncreative in themselves, they touch directly on those fundamental truths which I will now put before you.

A commonplace phrase is generally used to define the essence of music. As, for example, "Music is the art of sounds in the movement of time" or "in the combination of rhythm, melody and harmony", and similar phrases. Indeed, I once read: "Music consists of harmony and melody, the former for the left hand and the latter for the right." Also those well-meant poetic outpourings ("Music is a messenger from heaven", and its manifold variations) have little meaning, it is true, but they approach the root of our argument more closely than musical cliché-mongers.

These latter like to use names which have attained importance in our "Musical History"; whereas such names only sum
up the few sections of a clock we have constructed in order to
grasp the idea of time which otherwise would escape us. In
a similar relationship electricity was there from the beginning
also before we discovered it; just as everything still undiscovered was in being from the beginning, and is therefore also
now in being; so, too, the cosmic atmosphere teems with all
forms, motives and combinations of past and future music.

To me, a composer is like a gardener to whom a small portion
of a large piece of ground has been allotted for cultivation; it
falls to him to gather what grows on his soil, to arrange it, to
make a bouquet of it; and if he is very ambitious, to develop it
as a garden. It devolves on this gardener to collect and form that
which is in reach of his eyes, his arms—his power of differentiation. In the same way a mighty one, an anointed one, a
Bach, a Mozart, can only survey, manipulate and reveal a
portion of the whole flora of the earth; a tiny fragment of that
kingdom of blossoms which covers our planet, and of which an
enormous surface, partly too distant, partly undiscovered,
withdraws from the reach of the individual, even if he is a
giant. And yet the comparison is weak and insufficient because
the flora only covers the earth, while music, invisible and unheard, pervades and permeates a whole universe.

Even to the greatest giant, the circle in which his activity
unfolds must remain a limited one. However much he may
grasp, in relation to the infinity out of which he creates it, is
bound to be a tiny particle; just as the highest ascent takes us no
nearer to the sun. Inside this radius, ruled by one person and
restricted for him in time and place by the chances of his birth, the
individual mind feels especially drawn through a natural sympathy to particular points and cultures, while his nature is placed
in closer relationship with certain details, owing to similar distinctive qualities. The creative artist favours these points so much
that he gladly and frequently returns to them in his works, and
to such a degree that we others learn to recognise him in

them. In the same way we formulate the idea of love from the chance meeting with a few women (in fact pre-ordained) and we never conceive anything beyond these meetings; but love is the mutual attraction of mankind and things through endlessness and eternity. It is through the medium of a few composers familiar to us that we believe we have penetrated into the essence of music. What we really perceive of it are bits and formulas which, moreover, the lesser composers take over from the greater; until a new greater one perceives a hitherto hidden turning and this is the next step forward. This new one passes as a genius. In reality he owes his importance to the place and moment of his birth.

The essence of music is divined by a few single individuals; to the majority it is unknown or misunderstood. It is as if one wished to acquire a picture of the architecture of all times and countries from the few bricks we gather together.[1]

On the contrary such sporadic and fragmentary knowledge diminishes and confuses the true picture which, perhaps, might manifest itself to the inner perception of one of the elect in a moment of exalted vision.

If we listen, with deepest reverence and greatest admiration, to a movement of the almost divine Mozart (one of those spirits who, in many moments, came nearest to the essence of music), we must admit to ourselves that he had the following limitations, in so far as the expression of the original essence of music is concerned:

1. We are clearly conscious of the circle out of which his music is created, its dimensions, and its restriction in time and place.
2. The Master's sympathetic choice; what he chooses, what he neglects, what "suits" him personally.

[1] It is as if, out of an immense store, someone took as many treasures and provisions as he could grasp and carry. In his "haste" and depending on the certainty of grasp and eyes, much that is unsuitable will be taken; whereby "haste" may stand here for the short and uncertain length of life. I heap up these parallel examples on purpose, for they should help to clarify the meaning of this thesis.

3. The frequent repetition and accentuation of what he favours.

Whatever nature has given him to administer, and in whatever abundance, will be modified and fitted to his individuality by each of these three factors. So from the innumerable forms with which music surrounds us everywhere, the Master collects a limited choice for us, out of which he again draws a smaller choice; to which, in details (because he finds them pleasanter or more expressive), he frequently and gladly returns. Chosen for this mission it is not his merit but his destiny to work it out; whereas I consider it almost a crime if the unauthorised wish to walk in the same footsteps, just as it is not granted to the chosen one to step outside the limits of his own path. Let no one envy the genius, for it is to him that the most difficult and responsible part of the task falls, with no possibility of the distance which separates *us* from the essence of music ever being lessened by him.

It is not through inventing new resources or through individual cleverness that the distance will gradually be reduced, but through an unremitting effort to accumulate all previous achievements and those yet to be achieved; and at the same time we must continue to move away from that which is merely of individual importance and make it give way to the increasingly expansive and inexhaustible development of that which is of more general value. Just as the greater part of the heavens must for ever remain hidden to the astronomer, so shall we never grasp the essence of music completely; and the road that brings us nearer to the goal is extremely laborious to follow because those who are undistinguished in the realm of music dare to say and do just as much as the greatest leader. It is a road constantly obstructed by errors already made or even preached.

What is the essence of music? Not the virtuoso's performance, not the overture to Rienzi, not the theory of harmony, not the locally embellished folk-song of the various nations, developing behind brightly-painted boundary posts (in this case the separation into countries is already a denial of the essence of music). Even though every single one of these examples contains a tiny seed of the supreme whole, in so far as music includes all the elements, it is just because they do fall into sections that they will again be sub-divided, as if the vault of heaven were to be torn into little strips. What can the individual do in the face of such an abundance of material? From the depths of our hearts, therefore, let us be thankful to the select few who are privileged, at least on a small scale, through taste and form, inspiration and mastery, to set up a miniature model of that sphere from which all beauty and power flow to them. Mankind will never know the essence of music in its reality and entirety; would that they could at least arrive at distinguishing what does *not* belong to it! The "Guild",[1] more than anything, blocks the way, just as faith stands in opposition to dogma.

At times, and in rare cases, a mortal is by listening made aware of something immortal in the essence of music that melts in the hands as one tries to grasp it, is frozen as soon as one wishes to transplant it to the earth, is extinguished as soon as it is drawn through the darkness of our mentality. Yet enough still remains recognisable of its heavenly origin, and of all that is high, noble and translucent in what surrounds us and we are able to discern; it appears to us as the highest, noblest, and most translucent.

Music is not, as the poet says, an "ambassador" of heaven, but the ambassadors of heaven are those chosen ones on whom the high charge is laid to bring us single rays of the original light through immeasurable space. Hail to the prophets![2]

[1] At that time there were very many music "Guilds" or "Societies". They were sometimes formed to increase the number of performances for certain composer's works. [Translator's note.]

[2] I was told by a mutual friend that "Vom Wesen der Musik" was the last thing Busoni wrote. She took it down for him during his last illness and made the typescript for him. The same line of thought and vision can be followed in the "Realm of Music", "A Fairy-like Invention" and "The Essence of Music." [Translator's note.]

INDEX

INDEX

INDEX

INDEX

CATALOGUE OF DOVER BOOKS

Music

A GENERAL HISTORY OF MUSIC, Charles Burney. A detailed coverage of music from the Greeks up to 1789, with full information on all types of music: sacred and secular, vocal and instrumental, operatic and symphonic. Theory, notation, forms, instruments, innovators, composers, performers, typical and important works, and much more in an easy, entertaining style. Burney covered much of Europe and spoke with hundreds of authorities and composers so that this work is more than a compilation of records . . . it is a living work of careful and first-hand scholarship. Its account of thoroughbass (18th century) Italian music is probably still the best introduction on the subject. A recent NEW YORK TIMES review said, "Surprisingly few of Burney's statements have been invalidated by modern research . . . still of great value." Edited and corrected by Frank Mercer. 35 figures. Indices. 1915pp. 5⅜ x 8. 2 volumes. T36 The Set, Clothbound **$12.50**

A DICTIONARY OF HYMNOLOGY, John Julian. This exhaustive and scholarly work has become known as an invaluable source of hundreds of thousands of important and often difficult to obtain facts on the history and use of hymns in the western world. Everyone interested in hymns will be fascinated by the accounts of famous hymns and hymn writers and amazed by the amount of practical information he will find. More than 30,000 entries on individual hymns, giving authorship, date and circumstances of composition, publication, textual variations, translations, denominational and ritual usage, etc. Biographies of more than 9,000 hymn writers, and essays on important topics such as Christmas carols and children's hymns, and much other unusual and valuable information. A 200 page double-columned index of first lines — the largest in print. Total of 1786 pages in two reinforced clothbound volumes. 6¼ x 9¼. The set, T333 Clothbound **$17.50**

MUSIC IN MEDIEVAL BRITAIN, F. Ll. Harrison. The most thorough, up-to-date, and accurate treatment of the subject ever published, beautifully illustrated. Complete account of institutions and choirs; carols, masses, and motets; liturgy and plainsong; and polyphonic music from the Norman Conquest to the Reformation. Discusses the various schools of music and their reciprocal influences; the origin and development of new ritual forms; development and use of instruments; and new evidence on many problems of the period. Reproductions of scores, over 200 excerpts from medieval melodies. Rules of harmony and dissonance; influence of Continental styles; great composers (Dunstable, Cornysh, Fairfax, etc.); and much more. Register and index of more than 400 musicians. Index of titles. General Index. 225-item bibliography. 6 Appendices. xix + 491pp. 5⅝ x 8¾. T705 Clothbound **$10.00**

THE MUSIC OF SPAIN, Gilbert Chase. Only book in English to give concise, comprehensive account of Iberian music; new Chapter covers music since 1941. Victoria, Albéniz, Cabezón, Pedrell, Turina, hundreds of other composers; popular and folk music; the Gypsies; the guitar; dance, theatre, opera, with only extensive discussion in English of the Zarzuela; virtuosi such as Casals; much more. "Distinguished . . . readable," Saturday Review. 400-item bibliography. Index. 27 photos. 383pp. 5⅜ x 8. T549 Paperbound **$2.00**

ON STUDYING SINGING, Sergius Kagen. An intelligent method of voice-training, which leads you around pitfalls that waste your time, money, and effort. Exposes rigid, mechanical systems, baseless theories, deleterious exercises. "Logical, clear, convincing . . . dead right," Virgil Thomson, N.Y. Herald Tribune. "I recommend this volume highly," Maggie Teyte, Saturday Review. 119pp. 5⅜ x 8. T622 Paperbound **$1.25**

WILLIAM LAWES, M. Lefkowitz. This is the definitive work on Lawes, the versatile, prolific, and highly original "King's musician" of 17th century England. His life is reconstructed from original documents, and nearly every piece he ever wrote is examined and evaluated: his fantasias, pavans, violin "sonatas," lyra viol and bass viol suites, and music for harp and theorbo; and his songs, masques, and theater music to words by Herrick ("Gather Ye Rosebuds"), Jonson, Suckling, Shirley, and others. The author shows the innovations of dissonance, augmented triad, and other Italian influences Lawes helped introduce to England. List of Lawes' complete works and several complete scores by this major precursor of Purcell and the 18th century developments. Index. 5 Appendices. 52 musical excerpts, many never before in print. Bibliography. x + 320pp. 5⅜ x 8. T706 Clothbound **$10.00**

THE FUGUE IN BEETHOVEN'S PIANO MUSIC, J. V. Cockshoot. The first study of a neglected aspect of Beethoven's genius: his ability as a writer of fugues. Analyses of early studies and published works demonstrate his original and powerful contributions to composition. 34 works are examined, with 143 musical excerpts. For all pianists, teachers, students, and music-minded readers with a serious interest in Beethoven. Index. 93-item bibliography. Illustration of original score for "Fugue in C." xv + 212pp. 5⅝ x 8⅜. T704 Clothbound **$6.00**

Dover Classical Records

Now available directly to the public exclusively from Dover: top-quality recordings of fine classical music for only $2 per record! Almost all were released by major record companies to sell for $5 and $6. These recordings were issued under our imprint only after they had passed a severe critical test. We insisted upon:

First-rate music that is enjoyable, musically important and culturally significant.

First-rate performances, where the artists have carried out the composer's intentions, in which the music is alive, vigorous, played with understanding and sensitivity.

First-rate sound—clear, sonorous, fully balanced, crackle-free, whir-free.

Have in your home music by major composers, performed by such gifted musicians as Elsner, Gitlis, Wührer, Beveridge Webster, the Barchet Quartet, Gimpel, etc. Enthusiastically received when first released, many of these performances are definitive. The records are not seconds or remainders, but brand new pressings made on pure vinyl from carefully chosen master tapes. "All purpose" 12" monaural 33⅓ rpm records, they play equally well on hi-fi and stereo equipment. Fine music for discriminating music lovers, superlatively played, flawlessly recorded: there is no better way to build your library of recorded classical music at remarkable savings. There are no strings; this is not a come-on, not a club, forcing you to buy records you may not want in order to get a few at a lower price. Buy whatever records you want in any quantity, and never pay more than $2 each. Your obligation ends with your first purchase. And that's when ours begins. Dover's money-back guarantee allows you to return any record for any reason, even if you don't like the music, for a full, immediate refund—no questions asked.

MOZART: STRING QUARTETS: IN A (K. 464) AND C ("DISSONANT") (K. 465), Barchet Quartet. The final two of the famous Haydn Quartets, high-points in the history of music. The A Major was accepted with delight by Mozart's contemporaries, but the C Major, with its dissonant opening, aroused strong protest. Today, of course, the remarkable resolutions of the dissonances are recognized as major musical achievements. "Beautiful warm playing," MUSICAL AMERICA. "Two of Mozart's loveliest quartets in a distinguished performance," REV. OF RECORDED MUSIC. (Playing time 58 mins.)　　　　　HCR 5200 **$2.00**

MOZART: STRING QUARTETS: IN G (K. 80), D (K. 156), and C (K. 157), Barchet Quartet. The early chamber music of Mozart receives unfortunately little attention. First-rate music of the Italian school, it contains all the lightness and charm that belongs only to the youthful Mozart. This is currently the only separate source for the composer's work of this period. "Excellent," HIGH FIDELITY. "Filled with sunshine and youthful joy; played with verve, recorded sound live and brilliant," CHRISTIAN SCI. MONITOR. (playing time 51 mins.)　　　　　HCR 5201 **$2.00**

MOZART: SERENADES: #9 IN D ("POSTHORN") (K. 320), #6 IN D ("SERENATA NOTTURNA") (K. 239), Pro Musica Orch. of Stuttgart, under Edouard van Remoortel. For Mozart, the serenade was a highly effective form, since he could bring to it the immediacy and intimacy of chamber music as well as the free fantasy of larger group music. Both these serenades are distinguished by a playful, mischievous quality, a spirit perfectly captured in this fine performance. "A triumph, polished playing from the orchestra," HI FI MUSIC AT HOME. "Sound is rich and resonant, fidelity is wonderful," REV. OF RECORDED MUSIC. (Playing time 51 mins.)　　　　　HCR 5202 **$2.00**

MOZART: DIVERTIMENTO FOR VIOLIN, VIOLA AND CELLO IN E FLAT (K. 563); ADAGIO AND FUGUE IN F MINOR (K. 404a), Kehr Trio. The divertimento is one of Mozart's most beloved pieces, called by Einstein "the finest and most perfect trio ever heard." It is difficult to imagine a music lover who will not be delighted by it. This is the only recording of the lesser known Adagio and Fugue, written in 1782 and influenced by Bach's Well-Tempered Clavichord. "Extremely beautiful recording, strongly recommended," THE OBSERVER. "Superior to rival editions," HIGH FIDELITY. (Playing time 51 mins.)　　　　　HCR 5203 **$2.00**

SCHUMANN: KREISLERIANA (OPUS 16) AND FANTASIA IN C (OPUS 17), Vlado Perlemuter, Piano. The vigorous Romantic imagination and the remarkable emotional qualities of Schumann's piano music raise it to a special eminence in 19th-century creativity. Both these pieces are rooted to the composer's tortuous romance with his future wife, Clara, and both receive brilliant treatment at the hands of Vlado Perlemuter, Paris Conservatory, proclaimed by Alfred Cortot "not only a great virtuoso but also a great musician." "The best Kreisleriana to date," BILLBOARD. (Playing time 55 mins.)　　　　　HCR 5204 **$2.00**

CATALOGUE OF DOVER BOOKS

DONIZETTI, BETLY (LA CAPANNA SVIZZERA), Soloists of Compagnia del Teatro dell'Opera Comica di Roma, Societa del Quartetto, Rome, Chorus and Orch. Betly, a delightful one-act opera written in 1836, is similar in style and story to one of Donizetti's better-known operas, L'Elisir. Betly is lighthearted and farcical, with bright melodies and a freshness characteristic of the best of Donizetti. Libretto (English and Italian) included. "The chief honors go to Angela Tuccari who sings the title role, and the record is worth having for her alone," M. Rayment, GRAMOPHONE REC. REVIEW. "The interpretation . . . is excellent . . . This is a charming record which we recommend to lovers of little-known works," DISQUES.
HCR 5218 **$2.00**

ROSSINI: L'OCCASIONE FA IL LADRO (IL CAMBIO DELLA VALIGIA), Soloists of Compagnia del Teatro dell'Opera Comica di Roma, Societa del Quartetto, Rome, Chorus and Orch. A charming one-act opera buffa, this is one of the first works of Rossini's maturity, and it is filled with the wit, gaiety and sparkle that make his comic operas second only to Mozart's. Like other Rossini works, L'Occasione makes use of the theme of impersonation and attendant amusing confusions. This is the only recording of this important buffa. Full libretto (English and Italian) included. "A major rebirth, a stylish performance . . . the Roman recording engineers have outdone themselves," H. Weinstock, SAT. REVIEW. (Playing time 53 mins.)
HCR 5219 **$2.00**

DOWLAND: "FIRST BOOKE OF AYRES," Pro Musica Antiqua of Brussels, Safford Cape, Director. This is the first recording to include all 22 of the songs of this great collection, written by John Dowland, one of the most important writers of songs of 16th and 17th century England. The participation of the Brussels Pro Musica under Safford Cape insures scholarly accuracy and musical artistry. "Powerfully expressive and very beautiful," B. Haggin. "The musicianly singers . . . never fall below an impressive standard," Philip Miller. Text included. (Playing time 51 mins.)
HCR 5220 **$2.00**

FRENCH CHANSONS AND DANCES OF THE 16TH CENTURY, Pro Musica Antiqua of Brussels, Safford Cape, Director. A remarkable selection of 26 three- or four-part chansons and delightful dances from the French Golden Age—by such composers as Orlando Lasso, Crecquillon, Claude Gervaise, etc. Text and translation included. "Delightful, well-varied with respect to mood and to vocal and instrumental color," HIGH FIDELITY. "Performed with . . . discrimination and musical taste, full of melodic distinction and harmonic resource," Irving Kolodin. (Playing time 39 mins.)
HCR 5221 **$2.00**

GALUPPI: CONCERTI A QUATRO: #1 IN G MINOR, #2 IN G, #3 IN D, #4 IN C MINOR, #5 IN E FLAT, AND #6 IN B FLAT, Biffoli Quartet. During Baldassare Galuppi's lifetime, his instrumental music was widely renowned, and his contemporaries Mozart and Haydn thought highly of his work. These 6 concerti reflect his great ability; and they are among the most interesting compositions of the period. They are remarkable for their unusual combinations of timbres and for emotional elements that were only then beginning to be introduced into music. Performed by the well-known Biffoli Quartet, this is the only record devoted exclusively to Galuppi. (Playing time 47 mins.)
HCR 5222 **$2.00**

HAYDN: DIVERTIMENTI FOR WIND BAND, IN C; IN F; DIVERTIMENTO A NOVE STROMENTI IN C FOR STRINGS AND WIND INSTRUMENTS, reconstructed by H. C. Robbins Landon, performed by members of Vienna State Opera Orch.; MOZART DIVERTIMENTI IN C, III (K. 187) AND IV (K. 188), Salzburg Wind Ensemble. Robbins Landon discovered Haydn manuscripts in a Benedictine monastery in Lower Austria, edited them and restored their original instrumentation The result is this magnificent record. Two little-known divertimenti by Mozart—of great charm and appeal—are also included. None of this music is available elsewhere (Playing time 58 mins.)
HCR 5223 **$2.00**

PURCELL: TRIO SONATAS FROM "SONATAS OF FOUR PARTS" (1697): #9 IN F ("GOLDEN"), #7 IN C, #1 IN B MINOR, #10 IN D, #4 IN D MINOR, #2 IN E FLAT, AND #8 IN G MINOR, Giorgio Ciompi, and Werner Torkanowsky, Violins, Geo. Koutzen, Cello, and Herman Chessid, Harpsichord. These posthumously-published sonatas show Purcell at his most advanced and mature. They are certainly among the finest musical examples of pre-modern chamber music. Those not familiar with his instrumental music are well-advised to hear these outstanding pieces. "Performance sounds excellent," Harold Schonberg. "Some of the most noble and touching music known to anyone," AMERICAN RECORD GUIDE. (Playing time 58 mins.)
HCR 5224 **$2.00**

BARTOK: VIOLIN CONCERTO; SONATA FOR UNACCOMPANIED VIOLIN, Ivry Gitlis, Pro Musica of Vienna, under Hornstein. Both these works are outstanding examples of Bartok's final period, and they show his powers at their fullest. The Violin Concerto is, in the opinion of many authorities, Bartok's finest work, and the Sonata, his last work, is "a masterpiece" (F. Sackville West). "Wonderful, finest performance of both Bartok works I have ever heard," GRAMOPHONE. "Gitlis makes such potent and musical sense out of these works that I suspect many general music lovers (not otherwise in sympathy with modern music) will discover to their amazement that they like it. Exceptionally good sound," AUDITOR. (Playing time 54 mins.)
HCR 5211 **$2.00**

CATALOGUE OF DOVER BOOKS

**SCHUMANN: TRIOS #1 IN D MINOR (OPUS 63) AND #3 IN G MINOR (OPUS 110), Trio di Bol-
zano.** The fiery, romantic, melodic Trio #1 and the dramatic, seldom heard Trio #3 are both
movingly played by a fine chamber ensemble. No one personified Romanticism to the general
public of the 1840's more than did Robert Schumann, and among his most romantic works
are these trios for cello, violin and piano. "Ensemble and overall interpretation leave little
to be desired," HIGH FIDELITY. "An especially understanding performance," REV. OF RE-
CORDED MUSIC. (Playing time 54 mins.)   HCR 5205 **$2.00**

**SCHUBERT: QUINTET IN A ("TROUT") (OPUS 114), AND NOCTURNE IN E FLAT (OPUS 148),
Friedrich Wührer, Piano and Barchet Quartet.** If there is a single piece of chamber music
that is a universal favorite, it is probably Schubert's "Trout" Quintet. Delightful melody,
harmonic resources, musical exuberance are its characteristics. The Nocturne (played by
Wührer, Barchet, and Reimann) is an exquisite piece with a deceptively simple theme and
harmony. "The best Trout on the market—Wührer is a fine Viennese-style Schubertian, and his
spirit infects the Barchets," ATLANTIC MONTHLY. "Exquisitely recorded," ETUDE. (Playing
time 44 mins.)   HCR 5206 **$2.00**

SCHUBERT: PIANO SONATAS IN C MINOR AND B (OPUS 147), Friedrich Wührer. Schubert's
sonatas retain the structure of the classical form, but delight listeners with romantic freedom and a special melodic richness. The C Minor, one of the Three Grand Sonatas, is a
product of the composer's maturity. The B Major was not published until 15 years after his
death. "Remarkable interpretation, reproduction of the first rank," DISQUES. "A superb
pianist for music like this, musicianship, sweep, power, and an ability to integrate Schubert's
measures such as few pianists have had since Schnabel," Harold Schonberg. (Playing time
49 mins.)   HCR 5207 **$2.00**

**STRAVINSKY: VIOLIN CONCERTO IN D, Ivry Gitlis, Cologne Orchestra; DUO CONCERTANTE,
Ivry Gitlis, Violin, Charlotte Zelka, Piano, Cologne Orchestra; JEU DE CARTES, Bamberg Symphony, under Hollreiser.** Igor Stravinsky is probably the most important composer of this
century, and these three works are among the most significant of his neoclassical period of
the 30's. The Violin Concerto is one of the few modern classics. Jeu de Cartes, a ballet
score, bubbles with gaiety, color and melodiousness. "Imaginatively played and beautifully
recorded," E. T. Canby, HARPERS MAGAZINE. "Gitlis is excellent, Hollreiser beautifully
worked out," HIGH FIDELITY. (Playing time 55 mins.)   HCR 5208 **$2.00**

**GEMINIANI: SIX CONCERTI GROSSI, OPUS 3, Helma Elsner, Harpsichord, Barchet Quartet, Pro
Musica Orch. of Stuttgart, under Reinhardt.** Francesco Geminiani (1687-1762) has been redis-
covered in the same musical exploration that revealed Scarlatti, Vivaldi, and Corelli. In
form he is more sophisticated than the earlier Italians, but his music delights modern
listeners with its combination of contrapuntal techniques and the full harmonies and rich
melodies charcteristic of Italian music. This is the only recording of the six 1733 concerti:
D Major, B Flat Minor, E Minor, G Minor, E Minor (bis), and D Minor. "I warmly recommend
it, spacious, magnificent, I enjoyed every bar," C. Cudworth, RECORD NEWS. "Works of real
charm, recorded with understanding and style," ETUDE. (Playing time 52 mins.)
                                                                        HCR 5209 **$2.00**

**MODERN PIANO SONATAS: BARTOK: SONATA FOR PIANO; BLOCH: SONATA FOR PIANO (1935);
PROKOFIEV, PIANO SONATA #7 IN B FLAT ("STALINGRAD"); STRAVINSKY: PIANO SONATA
(1924), István Nádas, Piano.** Shows some of the major forces and directions in modern piano
music: Stravinsky's crisp austerity; Bartok's fusion of Hungarian folk motives; incisive di-
verse rhythms, and driving power; Bloch's distinctive emotional vigor; Prokofiev's brilliance
and melodic beauty couched in pre-Romantic forms. "A most interesting documentation of
the contemporary piano sonata. Nadas is a very good pianist." HIGH FIDELITY. (Playing time
59 mins.)   HCR 5215 **$2.00**

**VIVALDI: CONCERTI FOR FLUTE, VIOLIN, BASSOON, AND HARPSICHORD: #8 IN G MINOR, #21
IN F, #27 IN D, #7 IN D; SONATA #1 IN A MINOR, Gastone Tassinari, Renato Giangrandi,
Giorgio Semprini, Arlette Eggmann.** More than any other Baroque composer, Vivaldi moved
the concerto grosso closer to the solo concert we deem standard today. In these concerti he
wrote virtuosi music for the solo instruments, allowing each to introduce new material or
expand on musical ideas, creating tone colors unusual even for Vivaldi. As a result, this
record displays an entire area of his genius, offering some of his most brilliant music. Performed by a top-rank European group. (Playing time 45 mins.)   HCR 5216 **$2.00**

**LÜBECK: CANTATAS: HILF DEINEM VOLK; GOTT, WIE DEIN NAME, Stuttgart Choral Society,
Swabian Symphony Orch.; PRELUDES AND FUGUES IN C MINOR AND IN E, Eva Hölderlin,
Organ.** Vincent Lübeck (1654-1740), contemporary of Bach and Buxtehude, was one of the
great figures of the 18th-century North German school. These examples of Lübeck's few
surviving works indicate his power and brilliance. Voice and instrument lines in the cantatas
are strongly reminiscent of the organ: the preludes and fugues show the influence of Bach
and Buxtehude. This is the only recording of the superb cantatas. Text and translation included.
"Outstanding record," E. T. Canby, SAT. REVIEW. "Hölderlin's playing is exceptional," AM.
RECORD REVIEW. "Will make [Lübeck] many new friends," Philip Miller. (Playing time 37
mins.)   HCR 5217 **$2.00**

CATALOGUE OF DOVER BOOKS

J. S. BACH: PARTITAS FOR UNACCOMPANIED VIOLIN: #2 in D Minor and #3 in E, Bronislav Gimpel. Bach's works for unaccompanied violin fall within the same area that produced the Brandenburg Concerti, the Orchestral Suites, and the first part of the Well-Tempered Clavichord. The D Minor is considered one of Bach's masterpieces; the E Major is a buoyant work with exceptionally interesting bariolage effects. This is the first release of a truly memorable recording by Bronislav Gimpel, "as a violinist, the equal of the greatest" (P. Leron, in OPERA, Paris). (Playing time 53 mins.)   HCR 5212 **$2.00**

ROSSINI: QUARTETS FOR WOODWINDS: #1 IN F, #4 IN B FLAT, #5 IN D, AND #6 IN F, N. Y. Woodwind Quartet Members: S. Baron, Flute, J. Barrows, French Horn; B. Garfield, Bassoon; D. Glazer, Clarinet. Rossini's great genius was centered in the opera, but he also wrote a small amount of first-rate non-vocal music. Among these instrumental works, first place is usually given to the very interesting quartets. Of the three different surviving arrangements, this wind group version is the original, and this is the first recording of these works. "Each member of the group displays wonderful virtuosity when the music calls for it, at other times blending sensitively into the ensemble," HIGH FIDELITY. "Sheer delight," Philip Miller. (Playing time 45 mins.)   HCR 5214 **$2.00**

TELEMANN: THE GERMAN FANTASIAS FOR HARPSICHORD (#1-12), Helma Elsner. Until recently, Georg Philip Telemann (1681-1767) was one of the mysteriously neglected great men of music. Recently he has received the attention he deserved. He created music that delights modern listeners with its freshness and originality. These fantasias are free in form and reveal the intricacy of thorough bass music, the harmonic wealth of the "new music," and a distinctive melodic beauty. "This is another blessing of the contemporary LP output. Miss Elsner plays with considerable sensitivity and a great deal of understanding," REV. OF RECORDED MUSIC. "Fine recorded sound," Harold Schonberg. "Recommended warmly, very high quality," DISQUES. (Playing time 50 mins.)   HCR 5210 **$2.00**

Nova Recordings

In addition to our reprints of outstanding out-of-print records and American releases of first-rate foreign recordings, we have established our own new records. In order to keep every phase of their production under our own control, we have engaged musicians of world renown to play important music (for the most part unavailable elsewhere), have made use of the finest recording studios in New York, and have produced tapes equal to anything on the market, we believe. The first of these entirely new records are now available.

RAVEL: GASPARD DE LA NUIT, LE TOMBEAU DE COUPERIN, JEUX D'EAU, Beveridge Webster, Piano. Webster studied under Ravel and played his works in European recitals, often with Ravel's personal participation in the program. This record offers examples of the three major periods of Ravel's pianistic work, and is a must for any serious collector or music lover. (Playing time about 50 minutes).   Monaural HCR 5213 **$2.00**
                                                                                    Stereo HCR ST 7000 **$2.00**

EIGHTEENTH CENTURY FRENCH FLUTE MUSIC, Jean-Pierre Rampal, Flute, and Robert Veyron-Lacroix, Harpsichord. Contains Concerts Royaux #7 for Flute and Harpsichord in G Minor, Francois Couperin; Sonata dite l'Inconnue in G for Flute and Harpsichord, Michel de la Barre; Sonata #6 in A Minor, Michel Blavet; and Sonata in D Minor, Anne Danican-Philidor. In the opinion of many Rampal is the world's premier flutist. (Playing time about 45 minutes)
                                                                                    Monaural HCR 5238 **$2.00**
                                                                                    Stereo HCR ST 7001 **$2.00**

SCHUMANN: NOVELLETTEN (Opus 21), Beveridge Webster, Piano. Brilliantly played in this original recording by one of America's foremost keyboard performers. Connected Romantic pieces. Long a piano favorite. (Playing time about 45 minutes)
                                                                                    Monaural HCR 5239 **$2.00**
                                                                                    Stereo HCR ST 7002 **$2.00**

Language Books and Records

GERMAN: HOW TO SPEAK AND WRITE IT. AN INFORMAL CONVERSATIONAL METHOD FOR SELF STUDY, Joseph Rosenberg. Eminently useful for self study because of concentration on elementary stages of learning. Also provides teachers with remarkable variety of aids: 28 full- and double-page sketches with pertinent items numbered and identified in German and English; German proverbs, jokes; grammar, idiom studies; extensive practice exercises. The most interesting introduction to German available, full of amusing illustrations, photographs of cities and landmarks in German-speaking cities, cultural information subtly woven into conversational material. Includes summary of grammar, guide to letter writing, study guide to German literature by Dr. Richard Friedenthal. Index. 400 illustrations. 384pp. 5⅜ x 8½.
T271 Paperbound **$2.00**

FRENCH: HOW TO SPEAK AND WRITE IT. AN INFORMAL CONVERSATIONAL METHOD FOR SELF STUDY, Joseph Lemaitre. Even the absolute beginner can acquire a solid foundation for further study from this delightful elementary course. Photographs, sketches and drawings, sparkling colloquial conversations on a wide variety of topics (including French culture and custom), French sayings and quips, are some of aids used to demonstrate rather than merely describe the language. Thorough yet surprisingly entertaining approach, excellent for teaching and for self study. Comprehensive analysis of pronunciation, practice exercises and appendices of verb tables, additional vocabulary, other useful material. Index. Appendix. 400 illustrations. 416pp. 5⅜ x 8½.
T268 Paperbound **$2.00**

DICTIONARY OF SPOKEN SPANISH, Spanish-English, English-Spanish. Compiled from spoken Spanish, emphasizing idiom and colloquial usage in both Castilian and Latin-American. More than 16,000 entries containing over 25,000 idioms—the largest list of idiomatic constructions ever published. Complete sentences given, indexed under single words—language in immediately useable form, for travellers, businessmen, students, etc. 25 page introduction provides rapid survey of sounds, grammar, syntax, with full consideration of irregular verbs. Especially apt in modern treatment of phrases and structure. 17 page glossary gives translations of geographical names, money values, numbers, national holidays, important street signs, useful expressions of high frequency, plus unique 7 page glossary of Spanish and Spanish-American foods and dishes. Originally published as War Department Technical Manual TM 30-900. iv + 513pp. 5⅜ x 8.
T495 Paperbound **$1.75**

SPEAK MY LANGUAGE: SPANISH FOR YOUNG BEGINNERS, M. Ahlman, Z. Gilbert. Records provide one of the best, and most entertaining, methods of introducing a foreign language to children. Within the framework of a train trip from Portugal to Spain, an English-speaking child is introduced to Spanish by a native companion. (Adapted from a successful radio program of the N. Y. State Educational Department.) Though a continuous story, there are a dozen specific categories of expressions, including greetings, numbers, time, weather, food, clothes, family members, etc. Drill is combined with poetry and contextual use. Authentic background music is heard. An accompanying book enables a reader to follow the records, and includes a vocabulary of over 350 recorded expressions. Two 10″ 33⅓ records, total of 40 minutes. Book. 40 illustrations. 69pp. 5¼ x 10½.
T890 The set **$4.95**

AN ENGLISH-FRENCH-GERMAN-SPANISH WORD FREQUENCY DICTIONARY, H. S. Eaton. An indispensable language study aid, this is a semantic frequency list of the 6000 most frequently used words in 4 languages—24,000 words in all. The lists, based on concepts rather than words alone, and containing all modern, exact, and idiomatic vocabulary, are arranged side by side to form a unique 4-language dictionary. A simple key indicates the importance of the individual words within each language. Over 200 pages of separate indexes for each language enable you to locate individual words at a glance. Will help language teachers and students, authors of textbooks, grammars, and language tests to compare concepts in the various languages and to concentrate on basic vocabulary, avoiding uncommon and obsolete words. 2 Appendixes. xxi + 441pp. 6½ x 9¼.
T738 Paperbound **$2.45**

NEW RUSSIAN-ENGLISH AND ENGLISH-RUSSIAN DICTIONARY, M. A. O'Brien. Over 70,000 entries in the new orthography! Many idiomatic uses and colloquialisms which form the basis of actual speech. Irregular verbs, perfective and imperfective aspects, regular and irregular sound changes, and other features. One of the few dictionaries where accent changes within the conjugation of verbs and the declension of nouns are fully indicated. "One of the best," Prof. E. J. Simmons, Cornell. First names, geographical terms, bibliography, etc. 738pp. 4½ x 6¼.
T208 Paperbound **$2.00**

96 MOST USEFUL PHRASES FOR TOURISTS AND STUDENTS in English, French, Spanish, German, Italian. A handy folder you'll want to carry with you. How to say "Excuse me," "How much is it?", "Write it down, please," etc., in four foreign languages. Copies limited, no more than 1 to a customer.
FREE

Puzzles, Mathematical Recreations

SYMBOLIC LOGIC and THE GAME OF LOGIC, Lewis Carroll. "Symbolic Logic" is not concerned with modern symbolic logic, but is instead a collection of over 380 problems posed with charm and imagination, using the syllogism, and a fascinating diagrammatic method of drawing conclusions. In "The Game of Logic" Carroll's whimsical imagination devises a logical game played with 2 diagrams and counters (included) to manipulate hundreds of tricky syllogisms. The final section, "Hit or Miss" is a lagniappe of 101 additional puzzles in the delightful Carroll manner. Until this reprint edition, both of these books were rarities costing up to $15 each. Symbolic Logic: Index. xxxi + 199pp. The Game of Logic: 96pp. 2 vols. bound as one. 5⅜ x 8. T492 Paperbound **$1.50**

PILLOW PROBLEMS and A TANGLED TALE, Lewis Carroll. One of the rarest of all Carroll's works, "Pillow Problems" contains 72 original math puzzles, all typically ingenious. Particularly fascinating are Carroll's answers which remain exactly as he thought them out, reflecting his actual mental process. The problems in "A Tangled Tale" are in story form, originally appearing as a monthly magazine serial. Carroll not only gives the solutions, but uses answers sent in by readers to discuss wrong approaches and misleading paths, and grades them for insight. Both of these books were rarities until this edition, "Pillow Problems" costing up to $25, and "A Tangled Tale" $15. Pillow Problems: Preface and Introduction by Lewis Carroll. xx + 109pp. A Tangled Tale: 6 illustrations. 152pp. Two vols. bound as one. 5⅜ x 8. T493 Paperbound **$1.50**

AMUSEMENTS IN MATHEMATICS, Henry Ernest Dudeney. The foremost British originator of mathematical puzzles is always intriguing, witty, and paradoxical in this classic, one of the largest collections of mathematical amusements. More than 430 puzzles, problems, and paradoxes. Mazes and games, problems on number manipulation, unicursal and other route problems, puzzles on measuring, weighing, packing, age, kinship, chessboards, joiners', crossing river, plane figure dissection, and many others. Solutions. More than 450 illustrations. vii + 258pp. 5⅜ x 8. T473 Paperbound **$1.25**

THE CANTERBURY PUZZLES, Henry Dudeney. Chaucer's pilgrims set one another problems in story form. Also Adventures of the Puzzle Club, the Strange Escape of the King's Jester, the Monks of Riddlewell, the Squire's Christmas Puzzle Party, and others. All puzzles are original, based on dissecting plane figures, arithmetic, algebra, elementary calculus and other branches of mathematics, and purely logical ingenuity. "The limit of ingenuity and intricacy," The Observer. Over 110 puzzles. Full Solutions. 150 illustrations. vii + 225pp. 5⅜ x 8. T474 Paperbound **$1.25**

MATHEMATICAL EXCURSIONS, H. A. Merrill. Even if you hardly remember your high school math, you'll enjoy the 90 stimulating problems contained in this book and you will come to understand a great many mathematical principles with surprisingly little effort. Many useful shortcuts and diversions not generally known are included: division by inspection, Russian peasant multiplication, memory systems for pi, building odd and even magic squares, square roots by geometry, dyadic systems, and many more. Solutions to difficult problems. 50 illustrations. 145pp. 5⅜ x 8. T350 Paperbound **$1.00**

MAGIC SQUARES AND CUBES, W. S. Andrews. Only book-length treatment in English, a thorough non-technical description and analysis. Here are nasik, overlapping, pandiagonal, serrated squares; magic circles, cubes, spheres, rhombuses. Try your hand at 4-dimensional magical figures! Much unusual folklore and tradition included. High school algebra is sufficient. 754 diagrams and illustrations. viii + 419pp. 5⅜ x 8. T658 Paperbound **$1.85**

CALIBAN'S PROBLEM BOOK: MATHEMATICAL, INFERENTIAL AND CRYPTOGRAPHIC PUZZLES, H. Phillips (Caliban), S. T. Shovelton, G. S. Marshall. 105 ingenious problems by the greatest living creator of puzzles based on logic and inference. Rigorous, modern, piquant; reflecting their author's unusual personality, these intermediate and advanced puzzles all involve the ability to reason clearly through complex situations; some call for mathematical knowledge, ranging from algebra to number theory. Solutions. xi + 180pp. 5⅜ x 8. T736 Paperbound **$1.25**

MATHEMATICAL PUZZLES FOR BEGINNERS AND ENTHUSIASTS, G. Mott-Smith. 188 mathematical puzzles based on algebra, dissection of plane figures, permutations, and probability, that will test and improve your powers of inference and interpretation. The Odic Force, The Spider's Cousin, Ellipse Drawing, theory and strategy of card and board games like tit-tat-toe, go moku, salvo, and many others. 100 pages of detailed mathematical explanations. Appendix of primes, square roots, etc. 135 illustrations. 2nd revised edition. 248pp. 5⅜ x 8. T198 Paperbound **$1.00**

MATHEMAGIC, MAGIC PUZZLES, AND GAMES WITH NUMBERS, R. V. Heath. More than 60 new puzzles and stunts based on the properties of numbers. Easy techniques for multiplying large numbers mentally, revealing hidden numbers magically, finding the date of any day in any year, and dozens more. Over 30 pages devoted to magic squares, triangles, cubes, circles, etc. Edited by J. S. Meyer. 76 illustrations. 128pp. 5⅜ x 8. T110 Paperbound **$1.00**

CATALOGUE OF DOVER BOOKS

THE BOOK OF MODERN PUZZLES, G. L. Kaufman. A completely new series of puzzles as fascinating as crossword and deduction puzzles but based upon different principles and techniques. Simple 2-minute teasers, word labyrinths, design and pattern puzzles, logic and observation puzzles — over 150 braincrackers. Answers to all problems. 116 illustrations. 192pp. 5⅜ x 8.
T143 Paperbound **$1.00**

NEW WORD PUZZLES, G. L. Kaufman. 100 ENTIRELY NEW puzzles based on words and their combinations that will delight crossword puzzle, Scrabble and Jotto fans. Chess words, based on the moves of the chess king; design-onyms, symmetrical designs made of synonyms; rhymed double-crostics; syllable sentences; addle letter anagrams; alphagrams; linkograms; and many others all brand new. Full solutions. Space to work problems. 196 figures. vi + 122pp. 5⅜ x 8.
T344 Paperbound **$1.00**

MAZES AND LABYRINTHS: A BOOK OF PUZZLES, W. Shepherd. Mazes, formerly associated with mystery and ritual, are still among the most intriguing of intellectual puzzles. This is a novel and different collection of 50 amusements that embody the principle of the maze: mazes in the classical tradition; 3-dimensional, ribbon, and Möbius-strip mazes; hidden messages; spatial arrangements; etc.—almost all built on amusing story situations. 84 illustrations. Essay on maze psychology. Solutions. xv + 122pp. 5⅜ x 8.
T731 Paperbound **$1.00**

MAGIC TRICKS & CARD TRICKS, W. Jonson. Two books bound as one. 52 tricks with cards, 37 tricks with coins, bills, eggs, smoke, ribbons, slates, etc. Details on presentation, misdirection, and routining will help you master such famous tricks as the Changing Card, Card in the Pocket, Four Aces, Coin Through the Hand, Bill in the Egg, Afghan Bands, and over 75 others. If you follow the lucid exposition and key diagrams carefully, you will finish these two books with an astonishing mastery of magic. 106 figures. 224pp. 5⅜ x 8. T909 Paperbound **$1.00**

PANORAMA OF MAGIC, Milbourne Christopher. A profusely illustrated history of stage magic, a unique selection of prints and engravings from the author's private collection of magic memorabilia, the largest of its kind. Apparatus, stage settings and costumes; ingenious ads distributed by the performers and satiric broadsides passed around in the streets ridiculing pompous showmen; programs; decorative souvenirs. The lively text, by one of America's foremost professional magicians, is full of anecdotes about almost legendary wizards: Dede, the Egyptian; Philadelphia, the wonder-worker; Robert-Houdin, "the father of modern magic;" Harry Houdini; scores more. Altogether a pleasure package for anyone interested in magic, stage setting and design, ethnology, psychology, or simply in unusual people. A Dover original. 295 illustrations; 8 in full color. Index. viii + 216pp. 8⅜ x 11¼.
T774 Paperbound **$2.25**

HOUDINI ON MAGIC, Harry Houdini. One of the greatest magicians of modern times explains his most prized secrets. How locks are picked, with illustrated picks and skeleton keys; how a girl is sawed into twins; how to walk through a brick wall — Houdini's explanations of 44 stage tricks with many diagrams. Also included is a fascinating discussion of great magicians of the past and the story of his fight against fraudulent mediums and spiritualists. Edited by W.B. Gibson and M.N. Young. Bibliography. 155 figures, photos. xv + 280pp. 5⅜ x 8.
T384 Paperbound **$1.25**

MATHEMATICS, MAGIC AND MYSTERY, Martin Gardner. Why do card tricks work? How do magicians perform astonishing mathematical feats? How is stage mind-reading possible? This is the first book length study explaining the application of probability, set theory, theory of numbers, topology, etc., to achieve many startling tricks. Non-technical, accurate, detailed! 115 sections discuss tricks with cards, dice, coins, knots, geometrical vanishing illusions, how a Curry square "demonstrates" that the sum of the parts may be greater than the whole, and dozens of others. No sleight of hand necessary! 135 illustrations. xii + 174pp. 5⅜ x 8.
T335 Paperbound **$1.00**

EASY-TO-DO ENTERTAINMENTS AND DIVERSIONS WITH COINS, CARDS, STRING, PAPER AND MATCHES, R. M. Abraham. Over 300 tricks, games and puzzles will provide young readers with absorbing fun. Sections on card games; paper-folding; tricks with coins, matches and pieces of string; games for the agile; toy-making from common household objects; mathematical recreations; and 50 miscellaneous pastimes. Anyone in charge of groups of youngsters, including hard-pressed parents, and in need of suggestions on how to keep children sensibly amused and quietly content will find this book indispensable. Clear, simple text, copious number of delightful line drawings and illustrative diagrams. Originally titled "Winter Nights Entertainments." Introduction by Lord Baden Powell. 329 illustrations. v + 186pp. 5⅜ x 8½.
T921 Paperbound **$1.00**

STRING FIGURES AND HOW TO MAKE THEM, Caroline Furness Jayne. 107 string figures plus variations selected from the best primitive and modern examples developed by Navajo, Apache, pygmies of Africa, Eskimo, in Europe, Australia, China, etc. The most readily understandable, easy-to-follow book in English on perennially popular recreation. Crystal-clear exposition; step-by-step diagrams. Everyone from kindergarten children to adults looking for unusual diversion will be endlessly amused. Index. Bibliography. Introduction by A. C. Haddon. 17 full-page plates. 960 illustrations. xxiii + 401pp. 5⅜ x 8½.
T152 Paperbound **$2.00**

CATALOGUE OF DOVER BOOKS

Orientalia

ORIENTAL RELIGIONS IN ROMAN PAGANISM, F. Cumont. A study of the cultural meeting of east and west in the Early Roman Empire. It covers the most important eastern religions of the time from their first appearance in Rome, 204 B.C., when the Great Mother of the Gods was first brought over from Syria. The ecstatic cults of Syria and Phrygia — Cybele, Attis, Adonis, their orgies and mutilatory rites; the mysteries of Egypt — Serapis, Isis, Osiris, the dualism of Persia, the elevation of cosmic evil to equal stature with the deity, Mithra; worship of Hermes Trismegistus; Ishtar, Astarte; the magic of the ancient Near East, etc. Introduction. 55pp. of notes; extensive bibliography. Index. xxiv + 298pp. 5⅜ x 8.
T321 Paperbound **$1.75**

THE MYSTERIES OF MITHRA, F. Cumont. The definitive coverage of a great ideological struggle between the west and the orient in the first centuries of the Christian era. The origin of Mithraism, a Persian mystery religion, and its association with the Roman army is discussed in detail. Then utilizing fragmentary monuments and texts, in one of the greatest feats of scholarly detection, Dr. Cumont reconstructs the mystery teachings and secret doctrines, the hidden organization and cult of Mithra. Mithraic art is discussed, analyzed, and depicted in 70 illustrations. 239pp. 5⅜ x 8.
T323 Paperbound **$1.85**

CHRISTIAN AND ORIENTAL PHILOSOPHY OF ART, A. K. Coomaraswamy. A unique fusion of philosopher, orientalist, art historian, and linguist, the author discusses such matters as: the true function of aesthetics in art, the importance of symbolism, intellectual and philosophic backgrounds, the role of traditional culture in enriching art, common factors in all great art, the nature of medieval art, the nature of folklore, the beauty of mathematics, and similar topics. 2 illustrations. Bibliography. 148pp. 5⅜ x 8.
T378 Paperbound **$1.25**

TRANSFORMATION OF NATURE IN ART, A. K. Coomaraswamy. Unabridged reissue of a basic work upon Asiatic religious art and philosophy of religion. The theory of religious art in Asia and Medieval Europe (exemplified by Meister Eckhart) is analyzed and developed. Detailed consideration is given to Indian medieval aesthetic manuals, symbolic language in philosophy, the origin and use of images in India, and many other fascinating and little known topics. Glossaries of Sanskrit and Chinese terms. Bibliography. 41pp. of notes. 245pp. 5⅜ x 8.
T368 Paperbound **$1.75**

BUDDHIST LOGIC, F.Th. Stcherbatsky. A study of an important part of Buddhism usually ignored by other books on the subject: the Mahayana buddhistic logic of the school of Dignaga and his followers. First vol. devoted to history of Indian logic with Central Asian continuations, detailed exposition of Dignaga system, including theory of knowledge, the sensible world (causation, perception, ultimate reality) and mental world (judgment, inference, logical fallacies, the syllogism), reality of external world, and negation (law of contradiction, universals, dialectic). Vol. II contains translation of Dharmakirti's Nyayabindu with Dharmamottara's commentary. Appendices cover translations of Tibetan treatises on logic, Hindu attacks on Buddhist logic, etc. The basic work, one of the products of the great St. Petersburg school of Indian studies. Written clearly and with an awareness of Western philosophy and logic; meant for the Asian specialist and for the general reader with only a minimum of background. Vol. I, xii + 559pp. Vol. II, viii + 468pp. 5⅜ x 8½.
T955 Vol. I Paperbound **$2.35**
T956 Vol. II Paperbound **$2.35**
The set **$4.70**

THE TEXTS OF TAOISM. The first inexpensive edition of the complete James Legge translations of the Tao Te King and the writings of Chinese mystic Chuang Tse. Also contains several shorter treatises: the T'ai Shang Tractate of Actions and Their Retributions; the King Kang King, or Classic of Purity; the Yin Fu King, or Classic of the Harmony of the Seen and Unseen; the Yu Shu King, or Classic of the Pivot of Jade; and the Hsia Yung King, or Classic of the Directory for a Day. While there are other translations of the Tao Te King, this is the only translation of Chuang Tse and much of other material. Extensive introduction discusses differences between Taoism, Buddhism, Confucianism; authenticity and arrangement of Tao Te King and writings of Chuang Tse; the meaning of the Tao and basic tenets of Taoism; historical accounts of Lao-tse and followers; other pertinent matters. Clarifying notes incorporated into text. Originally published as Volumes 39, 40 of SACRED BOOKS OF THE EAST series, this has long been recognized as an indispensible collection. Sinologists, philosophers, historians of religion will of course be interested and anyone with an elementary course in Oriental religion or philosophy will understand and profit from these writings. Index. Appendix analyzing thought of Chuang Tse. Vol. I, xxiii + 396pp. Vol. II, viii + 340pp. 5⅜ x 8½.
T990 Vol. I Paperbound **$2.00**
T991 Vol. II Paperbound **$2.00**

CATALOGUE OF DOVER BOOKS

EPOCHS OF CHINESE AND JAPANESE ART, Ernest T. Fenollosa. Although this classic of art history was written before the archeological discovery of Shang and Chou civilizations, it is still in many respects the finest detailed study of Chinese and Japanese art available in English. It is very wide in range, covering sculpture, carving, painting, metal work, ceramics, textiles, graphic arts and other areas, and it considers both religious and secular art, including the Japanese woodcut. Its greatest strength, however, lies in its extremely full, detailed, insight-laden discussion of historical and cultural background, and in its analysis of the religious and philosophical implications of art works. It is also a brilliant stylistic achievement, written with enthusiasm and verve, which can be enjoyed and read with profit by both the Orientalist and the general reader who is interested in art. Index. Glossary of proper names. 242 illustrations. Total of 704 pages. 5⅜ x 8½.

T364-5 Two vol. set, paperbound **$5.00**

THE VEDANTA SUTRAS OF BADARAYANA WITH COMMENTARY BY SANKARACHARYA. The definitive translation of the consummation, foremost interpretation of Upanishads. Originally part of SACRED BOOKS OF THE EAST, this two-volume translation includes exhaustive commentary and exegesis by Sankara; 128-page introduction by translator, Prof. Thibaut, that discusses background, scope and purpose of the sutras, value and importance of Sankara's interpretation; copious footnotes providing further explanations. Every serious student of Indian religion or thought, philosophers, historians of religion should read these clear, accurate translations of documents central to development of important thought systems in the East. Unabridged republication of Volumes 34, 38 of the Sacred Books of the East. Translated by George Thibault. General index, index of quotations and of Sanskrit. Vol. I, cxxv + 448pp. Vol. II, iv + 506pp. 5⅜ x 8½.

T994 Vol. I Paperbound **$2.00**
T995 Vol. II Paperbound **$2.00**

THE UPANISHADS. The Max Müller translation of the twelve classical Upanishads available for the first time in an inexpensive format: Chandogya, Kena, Aitareya aranyaka and upanishad, Kaushitaki, Isa, Katha, Mundaka, Taittiriyaka Brhadaranyaka, Svetarasvatara. Prasna — all of the classical Upanishads of the Vedanta school—and the Maitriyana Upanishad. Originally volumes 1, 15 of SACRED BOOKS OF THE EAST series, this is still the most scholarly translation. Prof. Müller, probably most important Sanskritologist of nineteenth century, provided invaluable introduction that acquaints readers with history of Upanishad translations, age and chronology of texts, etc. and a preface that discusses their value to Western readers. Heavily annotated. Stimulating reading for anyone with even only a basic course background in Oriental philosophy, religion, necessary to all Indologists, philosophers, religious historians. Transliteration and pronunciation guide. Vol. I, ciii + 320pp. Vol. II, liii + 350pp.

T992 Vol. I Paperbound **$2.00**
T993 Vol. II Paperbound **$2.00**
The set **$4.00**

Dover publishes books on art, music, philosophy, literature, languages, history, social sciences, psychology, handcrafts, orientalia, puzzles and entertainments, chess, pets and gardens, books explaining science, intermediate and higher mathematics mathematical physics, engineering, biological sciences, earth sciences, classics of science, etc. Write to:

Dept. catrr.
Dover Publications, Inc.
180 Varick Street, N. Y. 14, N. Y.

26-100